Songs of a Psychopath (1)

Graeme Hetherington

Special Thanks

My thanks to Nicola Stevens, to whom without her timely intervention this book would never have happened!

Graeme Hetherington © 2026

graemehetherington.com

Printed and distributed by **IngramSpark**

ISBN: **978-1-7644974-0-4**

First Edition
2026

Dedication

For James McAuley

*'And alas, to have done time
Becomes itself a crime.'*

Acknowledgements

Coastlines, the Fellowship of Australian Writers (Northwest Tasmania) Strange and Marvelous Things, Ginninderra Press, Oxygen, Social Alternatives, Studio, The Mozzie, The Norma and Colin Knight Poetry Award First Prize 2025, First and Second Prize 2026.

Biography

Graeme Hetherington was born in Latrobe, Tasmania, in 1937. He spent his early childhood on the state's West Coast and attended the Rosebery and Zeehan state schools before moving to Launceston for boarding school and later to Hobart to study at the University of Tasmania. He went on to teach in the university's Classics Department for more than twenty-five years. During this time he developed a strong interest in European culture and later spent many years overseas fleshing out places and ideas he had taught about which were only thinly represented if at all in the Australian curriculum at the time.

In 2013 he returned to Tasmania to reconnect with his original roots. Much of his work reflects a lifelong restlessness and a search for a sense of home, and this theme of dislocation and uncertainty runs through his eleven previously published books of poetry.

Author's Introduction

Because the very coming into being of this epic text
spread arbitrarily over five volumes is closely connected
to the story of so much of my own life I feel obliged to
offer the reader a brief account of some of its key
elements in the interests of making the poem even more
accessible than it otherwise might be.

Born as an impractical 'useless arrangement' of convict
descent into the mining world of the West Coast of
Tasmania and being much teased, bullied and
nicknamed for my misfortune I was always going to be a
'poet' or some other equivalent of the victimised
crucified one. This was confirmed rather than modified
when I was 'rescued' and sent aged thirteen to be
educated at a boys' private boarding school after my
earlier more deeply formative years in the rough-and-
tumble of West Coast state schools.

Here I was totally misplaced as a working-class child
among the sons of original free-settlers who had settled
into comfortable, establishment ownership of the island
after wiping out most of the blacks. One can easily
imagine the conflicts and tensions that arose in me from
this juxtaposition! I had no inherited property to return
to on leaving school and my emotional underpinnings
had already been formed by salt-of-the-earth working-
class attachments.

Thus strongly motivated to matriculate and win my own
way in the world I came to the University of Tasmania
where I academically distinguished myself but because
of nit-picking rules and regulations I ended up as a
lecturer in a Classics Department rather than an English
Literature one. In the latter outfit my lack of Greek and

Latin was neither here nor there, but in the former gave me 'ring-in' status and damaged career prospects. This misplacement determined me to leave academia, and aspire to be the Dante of Australia!

Psychologically a mess and already in my twenties an alcoholic and unhappily married to an English ruling-caste type who'd transported my kind to VDL/Tas, as I called the isle, I was well and truly on the ropes, unable to handle profound feelings of disorientation and dislocation.

Then, in 1970, at the eleventh hour, enter James McAuley! I had known him in the 1960's as a charismatic party animal and Hobart's newly appointed professor of English, and been enthralled by his brilliant company, but only as one of many. But in 1970 he was diagnosed with terminal bowel cancer and the nature of my relationship with him changed.

Aged fifty and twenty years my senior he became something of a father figure to me. As Ganymede to Zeus, Enkidu to Gilgamesh, Patroclus to Achilles, I profited greatly at his side and his publication of five of my poems in 'Quadrant' in the five years before his death in 1976 radically advanced my destiny to write 'songs of a psychopath'. He even once playfully called me one as I recounted my lack of emotional nurturing as a child which is so often the cause of a lack of compassion for others. Not having been taught to love and care in childhood I was with my undeveloped conscience able to desert a mentally ill wife and daughters.

More pleasant, at boarding school I had won notoriety as the only one in the class to have learnt by heart the soliloquies of MacBeth. That, too, in its undefinable way seems, in retrospect, to have foreshadowed my fate to embrace poetry, and perhaps there have been other incidents, unrecognised, that are part and parcel of this seamless interweaving of life and the coming into being of this text so long in the making.

Then in 1986 after two failed marriages and as a disgruntled member of a classics department, I sold my university contract, thereby freeing myself to be a poet at large and Australia's very own Dante in exile, completing between that year and 1993 the first draft of a manuscript offering my comment on what has troubled me all my life: the appalling nature of existence. No one who knows the history of VDL/Tas will be surprised that the architecture of the poem is that of a seemingly never-ending prison.

And that is by no means the end of the saga. Abandoned in 1993 to give a third marriage a chance of success I only took this leviathan of a text up again in 2022, ten years after my third wife's death. It had been lying in wait behind the couch in a blue plastic brief case for about thirty years.

What drove me to open what might be a Pandora's box, or 'Graeme's Folly' as I jokingly called it whenever I decreasingly thought of it over the dwindling years? The answer is simple.

I had over all this time published eleven books of poetry of conventional size, 'slim volumes', as we say, and now found myself at a loss, fearful that my muse had died before me. I opened it and found it still possible to engage with. I had something to do, and the cobwebs blown off, began revising, polishing, adding to my interminable prison.

There remained though a seemingly insuperable problem. What I found physically, as well as some still interesting poems, was an unmanageable heap of A4 pages on which I had, in antiquated manner, typed up my manuscript. As well, I found that electric typewriter ribbons were now nowhere to be found.

For over two years I remained helpless in the face of this dilemma. How to gain control of the unwieldy mass, let alone market any of my abundant fruit? Then occurred the most timely of interventions in the form of Nicola Stevens, the second such to give me a chance to survive a formidable crisis.

It was a rescue attempt extraordinaire! As a new friend she procured a laptop for me, patiently taught me the skills of usage, interested herself in my literary project and now handles all the practicalities associated with beginning, because of the constraints of time, to self-publish the mammoth collection, leaving me free to endlessly refine. My acknowledgement of her as hand-maiden and 'surrogate daughter' need hardly be stated!

Such then, to date, is the history of this manuscript from its intangible, unknowable beginnings with me as a child unsuited to the West Coast of Tasmania to its more or less tangible form on a laptop.

Contents

Block One 1

Block Two 33

Block Three 63

Block Four 95

Block Five 127

Block Six 163

Bibliography 195

Block One

(1)

These short-back-and-sides sonnets built
Of strict octosyllabic lines,
Of beats just one less than the cat's
Reddened tails, are gaol cells I'd like
To break free from but can't. Bereft
Of a honeycomb's riches, I
Still hope readers will turn each key,
Visiting all to serve the time
Needed to get the hang of them,
And having digested the lot,
The blocks they've been arranged into,
The whole grey penitentiary
The isle was once, and this book is,
Be released to freedom at last!

(2)

Till thirteen years of age reared on
The constantly wet overcast
Hell's Gates' cannibalised West Coast
Among convict-descended folk
Government propaganda called
'Residuals', though we comprised
Sixty two percent, I escaped
As blotting paper sodden with
Memories, but only to return
At life's end to the East, where sun,
Instead of lightening, strengthens black
Squeezed out for poems, with manholes in
Ceilings thought of as trapdoors for
My ancestors to hurtle through.

(3)

(After Milton's 'Paradise Lost')

My matriarchal wowser-gran,
Shouting 'you devil!' dragged me from
Our sputtering one-valve wireless for
Using 'old crawler' Hell's Gates' gaol
Slang like 'sool' and 'skitch' to urge on
My obsessively loved blood-red,
Bruise-blue 'Demons' against 'The Saints'
Through static making my team ' Hounds
Of Hell', that got me sent to bed
Without tea for kicking her in
The shins, for knowing as a child
That when 'Goodies' and 'Baddies' fought
My heart was with the underdog,
With Lucifer thrown out by God.

(4)

'Bit of a devil, your old man'
Hell's Gates-formed blokes said with respect,
Though in his case mine was withheld
Since I judged him through mother's un-
Clouded stain-free New Zealand eyes,
Seeing him, of convict descent,
As Justice of the Peace unfit
To try others when he too sped,
Gambled and drank illegally,
A style inherited from his
Great-grandfather James Sparks sent out
For forgery, rising to be
A constable whose weakness for
Low life continued as before.

(5)

(For Mervyn Peake)

Reading Peake's 'Gormenghast' replete
With hellish, gothic images,
I thought it weird his name was in
Geoffrey Blainey's 'The Peaks Of Lyell',
Whose sulphur-reeking fumes I breathed
Could have Mephistophelised me,
Forming my Van Diemen's Land brain,
And even odder that the blood-
Infecting football ground on which
I skun knees should have been at near-
By Gormanston, explaining why
I once drank from a mug with Old
Nick depicted in flaming red
Saying 'God's dead, how can I help?'

(6)

Touched by, identifying with
Faust, Mephistopheles, Christ, Job,
The Virgin Mary, Magdalene,
Gilgamesh, Enkidu, St John,
Odysseus, Oedipus, God,
Achilles, Hector, Socrates,
I write aspiring to embrace
Wide-ranging possibilities,
Shed limited, birthright Hell's Gates'
Van Diemen's Land mythologies,
Their Hell's Gates' Pieman, Gabbett, Pearce,
Authoritarian Governors,
Bushrangers, poisoner-artists as
Role models, unfit to form souls.

(7)

My father's near-illiteracy
Painful to behold as he tried
To hide it making out headlines,
Or rarely struggled through a book
On Pharlap, Les Darcy, The Don,
Avoiding home-life for the pub
To slap other blokes' backs instead
Of giving me a hug as I
Watched brawling miners smash the posts
Of pub verandahs Friday nights,
His wriggling in discomfort when
It came to talk about forebears,
All meant childhood was shackled to
The deprivations of the past.

(8)

Unable to explain myself
From what little I knew about
My suppressed ancestry, I made
Up 'Aloyishus Featherstone'
Appropriately transported
For snatching a bulging purse from
Beneath a lifted petticoat
As a Duchess sat out a dance
At Windsor Castle or the like,
Imagining unearthing his
Poems stained by time done underneath
Rotting sugar sacks in a shack,
In bits and pieces waiting to
Be put together for the world.

(9)

Remembering my C of E
Masonic father breaking down,
His accusations of betrayal
When I announced I was engaged
To wed a Roman Catholic girl,
His jokes at the expense of 'Micks',
I've cast 'Aloyishus' as one,
Thinking of my forebears as priests
Who fed the London poor and were
Persecuted for their good works,
Preferring 'Paddies' as my friends,
Anything to be different from,
Revengefully defy my old
Man for failing me as a child.

(10)

Inspire me, Muse, to sing of my
Deep hatred for VDL/Tas,
My original island-home,
To explain why I've disowned kin,
The convict-blighted West Coast where,
Too sensitive for my own good
Bully-boys disfigured childhood,
Finding nothing to like in one
Who fled to Europe for his life
And stayed for over thirty years
In search of God-alone-knows-what,
Apart from Him, anywhere but
Remain on shores fatal to whales,
Seals, blacks, thylacines, transportees.

(11)

An habitue of the parks
In London, Athens, Madrid Rome,
I've come to get life off my chest
In Hania, Crete, to find out in
An epic where it all went wrong,
The public garden ideal as
An exercise yard for old lags,
A place to write, as Dante-like
I send to Hell foes, dead, alive,
To blame for my exile, a grey-
Fringed wistful gent twice split from 'Rule-
Britannia' sickly wives, and at
Long last at fifty retired from
Academia to create.

(12)

Where 'Aloyishus' poems begin
And mine end I can't always tell,
As in those likening Hobart Town's
Mount Wellington, its graceless form
To Thames-side hulks which I've not seen,
Or in some where The Iron Duke
Seems really to have been curled up,
Asleep in a dark heavy cloak
The night before he sent men to
Their Waterloo, as might an un-
Concerned, conscienceless psychopath,
And on those grounds I'll credit them
To my illustrious forebear,
Since he was there and I was not!

(13)

'During the Peninsular War
Goya captured the Iron Duke,
The sweat-filmed face and harried look
In gleam-cold eyes as he fights off
An impulse to personally kill,
That's hardened to indifference by
The time of Waterloo, and made
Hobart's mountain when I arrived
Him cloaked in sleep before we fought,
Relaxed, reclining as the might
Of England's unassailable
Aristocracy, its Empire,
Implacable, immovable
Above the tiny convict town'.

(14)

'No help given, as in the psalm,
Why should one in anguish of soul
Look to Mt Wellington that towers
Bully-like over Hobart Town
Cowering beneath foothills as if
Supplicating inhabitants
Have been kicked whimpering back down,
Especially as the blue-blood rock's
Present from all vantage points as
An inescapable mastiff
Hunting its quarry, cringing, squeezed
Between it and a choppy sea,
Barking that men not fit to die
At Waterloo were scum dumped here?'

(15)

Van Diemen's Land Tasmanian from
Hell's Gates, names evocative of
Demons, madness, Lucifer,
I see myself as their outgrowth,
Accursed and lonely as the isle
Between Australia and the Pole,
An Alcatraz, starkly bereft
Except for coastal scenery
That can't redeem the dull green rest
Of mostly monotonous scrub,
As painters, poets also don't,
Nor its past history's perpetual
Soul-corrupting horror show of
Just murdered blacks and convicts hanged.

(16)

The only island I know of
With madness built into its name,
Tasmania's grim beginnings stirred
The shit in human debris dumped,
Rare diaries, poems and letters home
Describing how the baleful light
And overwhelming deathly quiet
In hills as green as phlegm spat up,
In mountains blue and purple as
Bruises bloodcoats handed out to
Even the well-behaved thin-skinned
Like Aloyishus Featherstone,
Unhinged them unless drowned by rum
In unbelievable amounts.

(17)

Assigned to George Meredith's farm
On the isle's much milder East Coast,
Louisa Anne admired his poems
But couldn't save Featherstone from
His Fate to be sent by Sorell
To Hell's Gates in the harsh wild West
For debauching a servant girl,
Where he escaped with Gabbett, Pearce
To the indigestible bush,
Became a murderer, cannibal
Dining on mates' meat, gagging till
Like mother's milk he wolfed it down,
Explaining why I fear I'll kill,
Enjoy sucking blood from a cut.

(18)

Cursed be the name Van Diemen's Land!
In finding it the Dutch began
The processes begetting me,
A twinkle in their eye as down
The rough West Coast they sailed and killed
The black-browed albatross I wear
As frown-lines on my forehead to
Reproach them for my origins,
And later on the English who
By killing blacks and founding gaols
For my forebears transported there
Gave me a fouled birthright as all
I had to form me as a child,
My consciousness reeking of Hell.

(19)

As late as nineteen forty-five,
When I was eight and felt estranged,
The offspring of old crawlers lived
As derelicts in my hometown,
As ugly, maddened refugees
From life that wanted none of them,
So ingrained was defeat, their need
To be forever brutalised
And do dirt on themselves with drink.
They mumbled incoherently
And stumbled past me on the track,
No-hoper Vandemonians
With grog-filled fly-blown sugar sacks
A dog would not lie on to die.

(20)

Dogs nosing debris, vomit, turds
In run-down streets siesta-still,
The eerie de Chirico sense
Of unattached shadows that stretch
Surreally from corners and trip
Up in a heatwave's emptiness,
Its yawning somnolence, despair,
The sinister, waiting quietness
Of undisturbed dust and the stink
Of menstrual flow, yesterday's fish,
Have lured me spent to Hania for
Its provincial, backwater charm,
Kavafian sense of collapse,
Defeat salted with bitterness,
Echoing my defeated soul.

(21)

A flash bloke, if ever there was,
Who frequented casinos, drove
An imported stretch limousine,
This Tasmanian playboy as cash-
Flush painter-to-poor-poet be-
Friended me, took care of the tabs
At 'The Ball and Chain' restaurant,
But disproportionately made
Me pay when his wife asked him to
Remove rubbish from the car's back
Seat before I reclined there, quite
Accepting of being squeezed in
Till his 'he's from the Hell's Gates' West
And won't notice, let alone mind.'

(22)

I watch the Cretan Elders sway
In unison across the park,
Huge bellies chock-a-block with meat,
Who've come to sleep it off and dream
Of all the parachuting Krauts
They pitchforked, shot and clubbed to death.
I think of Kronos who devoured
His sons, of Ouranos who lost
His kingdom and his genitals
That foamed upon the hungry sea
Till Aphrodite struggled free,
Strained upwards to the sun as though
To embrace it with longing arms,
Love goddess born of hate and war.

(23)

To judge from certain letters sent
To his refined Mama back home,
A heightened sensitivity
Set Aloyishus well apart
From 'hirsute brutes with bloodshot eyes
Who'd hack the earth to bits for gleams
In hills already stripped and gashed
Like Christ's side by the Roman spear'.
A poet when he wasn't drunk
For forty days and forty nights
In order to escape the place
'As ugly as a possum pelt
A fire had singed unevenly',
He married and produced a son.

(24)

A stitcher of potato sacks
In Hobart's Female Factory,
Kate freed was drawn to the West
Up through the Derwent Valley towns
Of Gretna, Hamilton and Ouse.
Buxom domestic help in each
And sacked for drunkenness and theft
Till Aloyishus took her in,
She hitched her skirt up to the waist
To milk the bone-protrudent cows,
Knocked back the Bengal with the blokes
And qualified my pommy strain
With an authentic Tassie touch
I wear to this day like a wound.

(25)

Mum prim-and-proper, Dad a squirt
Eight inches short of my six feet,
The former stain-free, latter too
Clever to show his convict past,
I needed a town-bike, a bard
As forebears to make sense of my
Adventurously questing self,
Though Uncles Ron and Len as clerks
In timber mills and mines were caught
With fingers in the till and fired,
While cousin Cecil minced and lost
Post-masterships in seven towns,
And swigging from a bottle Aunt
Aileen sat legs apart and belched.

(26)

My sensuality engaged
By Hania's goats lifting tails to
Rub against anything to hand,
Lubricate and give Billy joy,
By thoughts of Pasiphae spread in
The crafted cow and longing for
Bull's thrusts and rush of hot sperm to
Engulf her womb and spawn the beast,
By Phaedra jerking on the rope
To have an orgasm as she
Fantasises about the chaste,
Prurient Hippolytus, I
Can only imagine could come
From Aloyishus and Kate Peach.

(27)

Displaced from the comparative
Refinements of New Zealand when
Her father had to leave and come
To Tasmania's West Coast for work
Because he had a history of
Burning down timber mills to cash
In on the insurance, my Aunt
Molly, my mother's sister, went
Insane imagining the boozed
Miners next door as fiends from Hell
Pestering her for favours, until
My old man, not able to stand
Her living with us, she died
Locked up in a Home for her kind.

(28)

The Aloyishus poems chart
His story of despair and hate
In 'Queenie', Tullah, Gormanston,
At Rosebery, Renison Bell, Zeehan,
All lumped together and despatched
As 'shanty towns a fart will sweep
Into shafts sunk for nothing found,
My sensibility outraged
By tanks and sacks serving to house
The wheezing gummy derelicts
Inflamed to madness if their plonk
Dries up on Saturday and they've
No means of getting to a pub's
'Sunday School' to allay DTs'.

(29)

'A' died obsessed with ugliness,
His poems full of 'scrawny gums',
'Naive, freckled, peasant-faced folk',
'Mean mouths, lipless as a lizard's',
'The flimsy, blow-away look of
Shacks, fences, leaning water tanks',
Old lags called 'lobster gobs' because
'Pink Englishness was boiled alive,
Sun ruining their eyes with squints,
Misery making them garrulous'.
Gum-booted in the one-room hut
He lived alone in at the end,
A soft green toe came off as well
As they prepared him for the grave.

(30)

Reported 'eaten in the bush'
Gave Aloyishus' freedom to
Breed a VDL child with Kate,
My chinless wonder of a great-
Grandad whose kids also were un-
Redeemed by any trace back to
The cultivated 'Featherstones',
Till I as throwback saved the show,
Treasuring, though Kate's part of me,
'A's' copy of 'The Odyssey'
The rats had had a go at in
The best-left-undescribed shack wind
Rain damp and heat had eaten of
But left his inscribed name intact.

(31)

Emotional necessity
Inspires me to see urine-stained
Hania Park leaves as scattered as
The Greek hero's trips round 'A's shack,
As now I need to imagine
Myself in workman's leather hob-
Nailed boots turned green from West Coast rain
Kicking another pile of bags
To release, not a snake as black
As rope miners use to winch ore,
But an annotated mildewed
'Iliad' that heralds with its
Companion a much kinder fate
For me than pick-and-shovel life.

(32)

Of 'Aloyishus', if they'd found
What 'crime' he'd been transported for,
My uncontaminated Gran,
A fierce wowser from Kiwiland,
Along with her daughter, my Mum,
Both despising Tasmania's West
And its Hell's Gates' connotations,
Would have exclaimed, living behind
Blinds pulled down tight in fear of Old
Nick peeping as they peed and pooed,
Undressed for beds that never warmed,
'Hanging's too good, he should have been
First drawn and quartered', cliches I
Recall from my accursed childhood.

(33)

Mutter, mutter, I'm a nutter,
Listen to me gag and stutter
From the gutter 'stop this utter
Nonsense, rubbish, chatter now I've
Come breathlessly spiralling down
Like a wounded butterfly, here,
There, levelling out from time to time,
Only to plunge again as Death
Inevitably has its way,
Bringing me squashed flat by a boot,
As though I'm just any old bug,
To float along a drain towards
An inescapable dark hole,
Gasping a poem out till the last.

(34)

At six feet three and eighteen stone,
Unnaturally large for then,
Thick-necked and with a bull's great head
No hangman's knot could jerk aside,
'A' had furrows scored across his
Impressive forehead, set when not
Suddenly raised as though surprised
And questioning of people's ways,
But delicate despite his size,
With shapely feet and slender hands,
Refined face just touched with a sneer
To keep the world at bay because
To let it in would imperil
Innate superiority.

(35)

Born-and-bred in Tasmania's West,
My illiterate Dad would have said
Of 'A's' verse if read out, 'what rot,
The ravings of a bloody pom,
And Jesus-eating Mick at that!',
But only behind his back, since,
Though sharing convict descent, he
Was still obsequious and hat-
Doffing towards the English as
His masters, a boot-licking Oz,
Tory-voting Alf Garnett, whose
Race-memory dictated he take,
When there was no risk, revenge for
Being kicked down the rabbit hole.

(36)

I often saw my father drunk,
But never nude like Noah's sons
That I might rush to shield his state,
Since unfailingly he locked doors
When using the toilet, bathroom,
Squeezed hard up against urinals
To render more private his part,
And so I hid behind a tree
To see his member as he peed
Thinking he was alone and safe,
A small white witchetty grub
Quite without the weightiness,
The patriarchal gravity
Of Abraham's seeding his race.

(37)

My mother would have blanched at 'A',
Married like her beneath himself
And suffering too Tasmania's West,
At bits and pieces of his poems
Blowing in from the shed for her
To accidentally come across:
'The bribed guards let whores board the hulk
To make the beast my cat-scarred back
Made even more monstrous', or this,
Less sensuously raw but still
Lacking enough in 'good taste' to
Outrage her sensibility:
'Thames slapping the sides of our gaol
As I playfully harlots' bums'.

(38)

If, defying need to suppress,
Female-factory, on-the-game
Bengal-addicted, thieving Kate
Had surfaced in our family lore,
My Kiwi-mother might have said:
'Too lowering of us to think
Of as a relative, her brood
Would have had dandruff, scabies, lice,
Smelt from sleeping three to a bed',
Though failing to exercise in
The West Coast's fearful Great Outdoors,
And having little else to do,
She grew to be as buxom as
The comely 'tart' held in contempt.

(39)

Neck forceps-scarred, I hurt my Mum
As thunder rolled and Horace Swift,
My bog-Irish quack-uncle with
Black Dog of Ulster wrapped around
His shoulders did his gloomy best
To separate me from the dark,
Her first-born 'with a head as big
As this 'ere football pumped up tight',
My Dad said as he mimed a kick,
While washing hands of me the Doc
Growled 'genius or fool, to find
A cap that fits will be his least
Of woes', nodding to Tassie mapped
Out on my vertebrae-crushed nape.

(40)

'The Women's Weekly', 'Sporting Globe'
Our printed fare, the Doc sent books
By Beatrice Potter for the mind
He thought might find room in my large
Noggin to flower despite stem fouled
By VDL/Tas engraved there,
Texts I tried to but couldn't read.
Compelled to lend them to my smart
Year-younger brother who knew how
Before he even started school,
While I repeated, deeply shamed,
Grade One, I much preferred to tear
Them up, be punished rather than
Have parents praise him even more.

(41)

An old doctor, he scandalised
The backward by wedding a young
Hospital nurse, my Aunty Luce,
Who wished to care for him as he
Had VDL/Tasmania's poor.
I saw him once as he lay ill,
Tidied, propped up for visitors,
Anointed with eau de cologne
To win round angels at The Gates.
He told me to take threepence from
His trousers hanging on a hook,
But pocket jingling like a ball-
And-chain I stole a handful of
Silver and never was found out.

(42)

My Fall was when wowser-Gran swooped,
Scruffing, dragging apart as I
In our woodshed upon the cat-
Shit-buried, urine-scented chips
Played Doctor Adam to Nurse Eve.
Our punishment was swift and sure,
Since soon in hospital to have
A clump of warts burnt off I threw
Up from the stench then heard my first
Love in the next ward scream as they,
Treating her for meningitis,
Lumbar-punched, trying to stop spine
Curving till she was head to heel,
Ixion bound to suffering's wheel.

(43)

I never again bowled my hoop
Down deserted Murchison Street
Beneath Mount Black in Rosebery
Without her bent in my mind's eye,
Exacerbated by a night-
Mare of us doubled up in Gran's
Round Sunday hat-box struggling to
Tear free from veil's fine clinging mesh,
To no avail until I woke,
Thrashing around and calling out,
Crying myself back into sleep,
Despite the risk, the horror should
The dream recur and I be bound
With her still in a writhing heap.

(44)

Forecasting doom in Hania's park,
A 'Cassandra', drugged, Elders said,
To ease her mental state instead
Of being shocked by ECT
Back to 'reality', reminds
Me of my first wife, English Rose
Psychiatrists obliged me to,
Since she so stubbornly refused,
Sign forms allowing them to run
High voltage through her head and blast
Endogenous Depression out,
Otherwise, they all affirmed,
Bullying to a man, she'd risk
Becoming irreversible.

(45)

Unable to forgive that I,
'A mere colonial' after all,
Could be so 'irresponsible',
'Insensitive' as to allow
Nurses to drag her 'terrified'
Into a 'torture chamber', clamp
'Clippers' to her 'Auschwitz-shaved head',
It ended in divorce, the loss
Of wife, daughters on their return
To the Old Dart', as though I had
Revengefully reversed history
To satisfy myself and kin
Who through transportation had lost
Their European heritage.

(46)

Right Wing Uni 'research' asserts
That Tassie's blacks were backward, in
Decline before the white man came,
That inherent stupidity,
Not syphilis, cholera, or
Smallpox and alcohol they brought,
Resulted in near-genocide,
While Leftists 'prove' the above were,
Along with massacres from greed
To acquire their best hunting grounds,
The cause of the catastrophe,
Both sides politicising to
Achieve their often doubtful ends
With truth always a casualty.

(47)

A Hell's-Gates' poem by 'A' I've pieced
Together tells of pack rape by
Cannibals, of his part played in
'Pinning the screaming lubra while
Travers de-flowering hoiked and spat
Satisfyingly in her face,
Then Pearce, Gabbett and I aroused
Had our way, while Brown, breaking down,
Disgusted, brained her on a tree',
The letters barely legible,
When, emphasising 'murderers'
He tore the page, concluding with
'My penis was the Roman sword
Thrust deep into Christ as He died'.

(48)

'A' tried to nail just how it felt
Living trapped in Van Diemen's Land,
What drove him to distraction most:
'It's similar to when you're forced
To write right-handed though inclined
Completely to the opposite,
Being made to walk upside down
On an already angry head,
Inducing fragmented, schizoid
Images such as viewing folk
Reduced to blackened gumtree stumps,
All their potential thwarted, stripped,
Forever in abeyance since
They've been so thoroughly misplaced

(49)

In Istanbul I saw lambs slain,
Decapitated in the snow
As substitutes for infidels,
Hearing them bleat still as blood dripped,
Printing mosaics, jewels like those
The Empress Theodora wore
Eight centuries before the Turks
Sacked Constantine's great eastern shrine,
That altogether with foes' heads
Heaped for disposal on trucks' trays
Brought to mind the concluding line
Of a poem I've imagined
'Aloyishus' could have composed:
'I shot the possums, not the blacks!!

(50)

'It's people, not the place that counts,
Screamed mad Rose, patience spent with my
'Childhood's surroundings structure us,
Environment determines all.
Tasmania's crazed unstable skies
Shot through with gleaming pewter snarl
Like watchdogs' bared fangs at The Neck,
And walking through dense tangled scrub
Reminds me of dragged ball-and-chain,
Charred trees the tribes of blacks wiped out
By free settlers with convict slaves,
While mugshots, faces gaunt from hate
Bring back the whistle of the cat
That's knotted tightly in my heart.'

(51)

It started with the dregs I'd drink
In rum and sherry bottles tossed
By Jack Grubb all around his shack,
And sometimes from frayed hessian sacks
Cheap Brandivino rolled intact
As he or others of his ilk
Fell from the school bus bringing them
On Pension Day back home with us,
From Zeehan to Renison Bell
Where I became addicted to
Grog's warmth thawing hate in my heart,
The way anxiety was replaced
And tension's steely line dissolved
Without the sudden snap I feared.

(52)

Identifying with the scum
Who lived below ships' waterlines
Before they made it through Hell's Gates
And later on to West Coast towns
As derelicts 'The System' spawned,
And recognising in myself
The archetypal philanderer,
The rat who steals another's wife,
As pretty-boy Paris I've lived
As gigolo in Athens, Crete,
Exploiting disillusioned well-
Heeled, lonely divorcees fetched up
There middle-aged as expats with
An alcohol problem to share.

(53)

Governor of VDL/Tas, Black's
A stick and not a whisky man,
His sword not ceremonious
As in and out it thrusts despite
Unpromising beginnings at
Launceston Church Grammar School, where,
He from the right side of the track,
And I his Hell's Gates' counterpart,
Were feminised in different ways,
His bad back in a corset, while,
Nicknamed 'Blossom' I sat behind
And kicked him there, not knowing then
It was revenge for floggings his
Kind had sentenced my kindred to.

(54)

In Hania's park I recalled Rose,
Depressed and weeping, as on edge,
Defensively I showed her round
The scaled-down mimicked Georgian streets
Of Battery Point in Hobart Town,
My new pom wife who aped the Royals,
Whose kind transported convicts there,
Naïve in my hope that we'd live
Harmoniously together when
I'd returned, having once escaped,
My tail between my legs to teach
The Classics shamefully again
In translation to felons' spawn
Though I myself was one of them

(55)

Rose manic, face crumbling, red
As arrow-patterned Battery Point
Bricks, as she sobbed expressing her
Harsh aristocratic response:
'You can't expect a Surrey girl
From Leatherhead, a Londoner,
Whose family seat was called 'The Glade',
To settle in a dwarf's twee house
Belonging more to toyland-town
Than any capital I've known,
Mount Wellington darkening as I
Look and smell evil in the air
You didn't mention in your need
To return and entice me here!'

(56)

Backyard abortions in her teens
Combined with Hobart's sinister
Guilt-ridden atmosphere and shame
Embodied in the hare-lipped folk,
Depressed, run-down and ill-at-ease,
Who still walk as though ball and chained,
Creep dutifully to work by nine,
Unhinged Rose almost straight away:
'What little you told me about
Van Diemen's Land's grim origins
In London as you courted me
I took then with a grain of salt,
But now you're poisoning my food
As Thomas Wainewright might have done!'

(57)

An 'Aloyishus' poem proclaims:
'As well as classicist and priest,
Ny father was a renegade
Whose hatred of the arrogant
Pom ruling class was passed to me
Who loathe the great-arsed English girls
For thumping up and down upon
Their ill-fed mounts until they fall,
Backs broken as they're forced to clear
Obstacles even if they've baulked,
And whom I'm tempted to, but don't,
Ride whimpering into the ground,
Their imperiousness reduced
To a humble-pie mouthful of dirt.

(58)

'The prison Commandant's wife rode
Around the Compound I'd helped build,
Astride to titillate inmates,
Or haughtily side-saddled down
The John Price Avenue Bill Booth
Had lined with English trees, such was
His hatred of the 'unkempt' gums
He said looked as 'undisciplined'
As convicts he'd vowed to 'correct',
Wrote 'A' before being shipped from
Port Arthur to Hell's Gates, unless
It was the other way around,
Poem's provenance a casualty
Beneath fly-blown potato sacks.

(59)

'The Commandant, O'Hara-Booth,
In company with his wife was made
Miserable by the Governor's un-
Announced, but all too frequent trips
From Hobart Town to find a sign
That his pet project had declined,
'Hunting for specks of dust', they moaned,
Obliged to give him lunch each time
At a moment's notice beneath
His favourite imported oak tree,
Put up with him gloating at chained
Convicts installing The Walkway's
Roaring stone lions he patted on
Arrival and when taking leave.'

(60)

As Gilgamesh on the decease
Of his friend set out on a quest
For immortality, so I
On mine went forth to seek the same
Through poetry, aware I was
Off to a rotten start, my soul,
Already besmirched by childhood
Spent in the shadow of Mount Black
And Hell's Gates, and also in
My wowser-gran's that grew out of
Her already in mourning clothes,
Unable still to contemplate,
Unless through a glass darkly, Greek
Philosophy's eternal truths.

Block Two

(1)

An alcoholic at nineteen
In need of funds to get wiped out,
Just like the blacks, one vac I dug
Foundations for a 'looney bin'
With 'Bruiser' shaking from the grog
And 'fucked' if he'd 'bust guts out for
Pay lower than a mongrel dog',
Who couldn't wield his shovel long
In heavy clay shot through with stones
Without a bitter, hissing stream
Of 'rotten cunts' until he broke
The handle, splintering his crotch
And drying out in hospital
On workers 'compo' for a year.

(2)

A half-caste past the pension age,
Joe Nettup was my other mate
At Lachlan Park in '58,
Near-blindness leading him to fear
'Getting the bullet', and why he
Never bludged, touching hat to all
And sundry, slavish to the point
Of washing pick and shovel clean,
Bowing low to the boss who gave
Him without let-up a hard time,
While 'Blue' and 'Curl' fresh out of gaol
Called him 'a bag of shit' and prayed
To God as 'Huey' to send down
The rain and free them for the piss.

(3)

My need to have 'Aloyishus'
Imagined as kin to explain
My difference from my father's side
Of low-brow convict ancestors
Also stems from failure to live
Happily with traits from my cold
Reclusively prone mother's New
Zealand family, its matriarch
Fanatically Methodist, while
One daughter was 'schizoid', a son
'Missing' and rumoured to be 'bad',
The sire a 'pyromaniac',
All part of my craving to be
Ennobled by a 'Featherstone'.

(4)

'What tommy rot!' was my old man's
Impatient response as in rage
I denied him his fatherhood,
Especially when late for Lodge in
Outgrown faded black dinner suit
And apron coloured blue and gold
'To ride the goat and tickle palms',
Secret rituals in a black book
Temptingly 'hidden' near the phone,
While mother, disdaining the scene,
And waiting for him to be gone,
Squeezed in an easy chair behind
The clothes horse to thaw out before
A mean weak fine, blocking me out.

(5)

The child of Aloyishus then,
My would-be ancestor enlarged
From reading Robson, Reynolds, Hughes,
Boyce, Porter, Richardson, Clarke, Koch
To help me tolerate a past
My father, ashamed, never aired,
That bored my 'stain'-free mother, but
Which drove me to put flesh on to
Explain my inborn hatred of
It as just convicts, murdered blacks,
My inability to love,
Identify with born-and-bred
Native island whites, though like them
I drank heavily to escape.

(6)

Our mother tried to keep us safe
From gangs of shanghai-toting sub-
Specie boys who smashed street lights, broke
Into the school and trashed classrooms
Where teachers caned, flogged as of old.
Two brothers raised to think ourselves
Better than other West Coast kids,
We weren't allowed out much and learned
To crucify each other, see
The unexplored wilderness as
More hostile than it really was,
A fearful void I filled up with
Murderers and cannibalism
Adults sheepishly grinned about.

(7)

Throwback, trapped in a time- warp, it's
Been my lot to live half-dead in
The isle's West steeped in Hell's Gates' lore,
Then in a kind of fury try
To shake it off, exploding out
Of Tas and fetching up in Greece,
A crippled outgrowth of an act
Of white supremacy, more at
Home in my mind with Gabbett than
'The Lily Prince' in Crete, or with
A Byzantine Christ, who in His
Soul voyaged deeper, further than
Will any spaceship ever through
The never-ending, thickening dark.

(8)

The tone in public life acquired
From bigots, crooks, incompetents,
Adulterers and psychopaths,
Van Diemen's Land was also lost
To rampant alcoholism
Among discontented white trash
Who didn't come of their free will,
To viciousness, back-biting, greed,
Murdering of blacks whose shadows sweep
Across the hills each time a cloud
Obscures the sun, the best men weak
Like Governor Franklin ruled by Jane
Who reduced Nature's snakes but failed
Against the swarming human kind.

(9)

'No monumental buildings, streets
That cobblestoned give depth to life,
No meaning in the black man's art
Our foreign sensibilities
Can tune into and be enriched,
The European loses all
Except a life he doesn't want
Devoid of his rich heritage,
And nothing white invaders make
In architecture, music, verse,
Painting, will ever harmonise,
Go naturally with a land
Only the natives understand',
Wrote 'Aloyishus', summing up.

(10)

'VDL dismantles those with
A European consciousness
Inherited from centuries
Of celebrating Easter when
The season is appropriate
For the ritual of re-birth,
Christmas snow confirming the babe
In purity', wrote 'A' in heart-
Felt vein, 'the punishment of such
An exile disproportionate
For mostly petty crime, while gaol,
Cat-o-nine, hanging, ball-and-chain
Into the bargain were too much
And broke instead of cured a man'.

(11)

The generations pass and still
Tasmania seems a weird outgrowth,
The folk neurotically disturbed
As unaware they dwell, not live
Truly engaged, their deepest selves
Unrelated, not rooted in
The all- but- wiped-out blacks' homeland,
The houses looking blown about
As driving rains and winds unnail
The sheets of tin, buckle the boards,
Swipe, hit full-on, prise apart till
The paling fences fan like wings
Of wet-through, sad grey crippled birds
That can't get off the muddy ground.

(12)

'I free you, live in Greece and write!',
Screamed Eve, second pom wife, Rose back
In England with our daughters, lost,
Irreplacable now the World's
First Mum ironically had tied,
Irreversibly, her tubes, but
Responsibly, to not risk kids
With her hereditary disease,
Incensed I had another Muse,
Scorning to envy, compete with,
More proof, if needed, of my deep
But unresolved love-hatred for
The Old Dart, culturally embraced,
Historically the foe.

(13)

Cavalierly, I agreed to
Live at large without Evelyn
Rather than passively wait for
Death in Hobart's suburbia,
Collecting each morning from some
Pest-eaten lawn 'The Mercury'
That never landed with the grace
Of messenger-god Hermes, but rolled-
Up bounced about till stuck in mud
Reflective of the daily news,
Burst wrapper, front page print a mess
Anticipating toilet use,
Qualifying the bright note struck
By an otherwise sparkling frost.

(14)

Resentful of sarcasm from
Housemaster 'Tadpole' Sorell, kin
Of the founder of Hell's Gates, his
'For a boy from there I'm surprised
At how well you're behaving here',
Topping up loathing of his kind,
Since I was born with hidden hate
Of condescension from on high,
For the inane, infantile tongue-
In-cheek praise of 'real progress made
In distant far-flung realms such as
Tasmania', complicating things
When I wed a ruling-caste pom
Just to demonstrate that I could.

(15)

McAuley, Harwood, Porter, Koch
And I in this have got it right:
Van Diemen's Land was demon-cursed,
Evil distilled into a speck
Upon the water's face, that seeped
Ineradicably into
The fibre of Tasmanians' souls,
Concentrated convictism,
A near-exterminated race,
Sub-specie, low-life sealers who
With whalers bred from blacks a class
So disdained by the ruling caste
They never had a chance in life,
Setting the tone for evermore.

(16)

Two lost aunts on my mother's side,
One mad, the other vanished from
The world without a by-your-leave,
Their brother left in Kiwi Land
Made up of studied silences
In answer to all questions asked,
An uncle sacked for petty theft
My father bowed his head about,
And one by marriage for the same
Stock-in-trade Van Diemen's Land crime,
Another haemorrhaging from drink,
And cousins, too close for comfort,
Spastic and queer, explain my need
For 'Aloyishus Featherstone'.

(17)

Accursed with under-privileged genes
Arising from VDL used
As a dumping ground for the worst,
I wear a prison-grey tracksuit,
Collar too low to hide my born-
To-be-hanged birthmark, a map of
Tassie forceps left on my neck,
This, with a mug-shot face, cropped hair
Leading to lost wives, kids, homes, work,
Any ambition save the need
To understand my failure to
Shake off a past I still wear like
My skin despite convicts not trans-
Ported since eighteen-fifty three!

(18)

Prof Paddy James, true poet of
Persecuted Irish background,
With hooded hangman's teasing eyes,
Who'd kissed the Blarney Stone and won
My limited supply of love,
Assisted, Svengali-like at
The despatch of mad pommy Rose,
Sent more so wondering if my wild,
Extravagant, besotted praise
Of him, his teaching, verse, girlfriends,
Capacity for alcohol,
Seeming success in life, was not
A homosexual affair,
Which it, deceptively, was not.

(19)

Released from hospital dried out
And partying on ginger ale
Hoping its cognac colour would
Fox peers who scorned my giving up
Booze to cure pancreatitis,
When Pad, who'd come to Tassie for
A holiday from Cold War strife,
Courageously stepped in and stopped
The urgers from threatening my will,
Adding a dimension to my
Reverential regard for him
Intuiting that one drink in
My case would lead to countless more
And perhaps death from the disease.

(20)

Famed for solving the Orr Case that
Made teaching philosophy at
Tas Uni possible again,
For hoaxing modernists with verse
Assembled from newspaper prose,
For switching from crazed Left to Right,
From wishy-washy Protestant
To Catholic in soul-searching poems,
Pad as a Cold War Warrior,
Who with Santa Maria helped
To weaken Labor in thrall to
The Reds and thus rout evil, was
My hero, the role model real
Ill-fated father failed to be.

(21)

Of mythical proportions, face
Creased not only by sleeplessness
Bringing poems to heel, but like
Auden's from shouldering the world,
Pad's coming to the backward isle
Was inspirational for me
Who found him charismatic, one
For whom folk stood up for without
Demur when he entered a room,
His feline elegance and grace
So natural that even when
Eating an apple waiting for
A bus true style was on display
To mystify and wonder at.

(22)

Heart, shield, female's triangle scored
Upon my neck, the birthmark's shape
A map of VDL/Tas too,
That adhering there weakens me,
As a leaf did stuck to Siegfried,
Thetis's hand Achille's heel
As she tried to immortalise,
Holding him in the river Styx,
My vulnerable spot striking when
It clicks like shots fired off against
My ears, startling me wide awake
To jerk and snap it back in place
In case it's out of joint, as in
Hanging, the island's famed forte.

(23)

Bright winter morning, a hoarfrost
An unobstructed sun played with,
The first day ever in the world,
When Renison deserved the Bell,
Making it a beautiful name
As I sat with men in a closed
Carriage on the way to mine tin
When someone signalled a fart with
'Dear Jesus, who opened their crib?,
Wafting a foul smell that enforced
The low-grade humour, and I thought
How convicts setting out to work
In threadbare clothes would not have joked
In prospect of cold taking hold.

(24)

'No-hoper Vandemonians
Exemplify the ancient Greek
'Count no man happy till he's dead',
Since they're unable to admit
To being so without a snarl,
A surliness that colours all,
As though unchained they deeply know
Good fortune doesn't last for long.
I see it in the shoulders slumped
And hear it in the scuffing boots,
The adenoidal voices that
Deferentially whine when they
Must speak to anyone of rank,'
Wrote Aloyishus in despair.

(25)

Humankind's tragedy persists,
Since never in our hearts will we
Feel truly comfortable with
Systems destructive of the race,
That show a scant compassion, can't
Organise food to end famines,
Adjust genes to abolish war,
That foul our shared and only nest,
Preach tolerance, honesty, love
Despite behaviour showing words
Have little or no worth, 'sincere'
Handshakes not to be trusted when
It's impossible to know what
Goes on behind another's eyes!

(26)

'As antidote to Kate destroyed
By Bengal rum and scum, I seek',
Wrote 'A' in exasperation,
'A woman whole in body, mind,
For one impossible to find,
Aware their texture is all wrong,
That every time a local speaks,
Comes slummocking in slippers to
The shed through mud to milk the cows,
Or gives a tooth-gapped gormless grin,
My hope makes little sense, yet still
Idealistic, I need against
Insuperable odds to try
My luck with Hell's Gates' West Coast stock!'

(27)

'My ulcerated toe won't heal',
Penned 'Aloyishus' in a mess
At Renison Bell after Kate
Died king-hit in a miners' brawl
She tried to break up with a chair.
'It's gangrenous and sticks to socks
I wear with gumboots in the heat
Along the overgrown track
Snakes lie in waiting on in case
I trip and spill the milk they love.
Should I die with black rubber glued,
Melted by then into the flesh,
I hope they'll carefully cut, not pull
It roughly off with foot in tow!'

(28)

A make-up artist with my nose
I popped a pimple on and caused
A third hole that's not healed in months,
Creating the illusion there's
No pit beneath the cream to draw
Another's sharp cruel eyes to probe,
I think of spirochaetes in blood
Waiting screw-like to strike the brain,
As with Mann's Leverkuhn, of how
Once walking with a friend I saw
A maggot writhing near his shoe
And glanced suspiciously at him,
Of Richlieu whose fundament
Was slightly torn and wouldn't mend.

(29)

I think too of depressed mad Rose
I had to tell to take a bath,
Who kept a tampon in for days
Then lured me to have sex with her,
Of Evelyn's bronchiectasis,
Her lobectomy leading to
A permanent infection in
Her respiratory system, and ask
If childhood on the West Coast where
Everything rotted in the rain
Explains my sensuality,
Attraction to such women, both
English, who seemed to love their own
Body odour above all else.

(30)

A stick that crumbled as I leant,
Assuming it would take my weight
Among the dying olive trees
My run-down flat in tired Hania
Looks onto through cracked dusty panes,
Made me think of deserted mines,
Of unfenced rubbish-tip shafts worked
By golden maggot-tailed blowflies,
Of rusting bits of dumped machines,
Black mullock mounds and sheets of tin
Bad weather had loosened on shacks
Whose rain-rotted frames couldn't take
Another nail to save them from
Impending disintegration.

(31)

Fire burning on the water's face
Of Tassie's Lake St. Clair where Pearce
The Hell's Gates' cannibal was crowned
By Aloyishus' with primrose
Before they split, one to be hanged,
The other sentenced till old age
To bend his scarred back in the mines,
I tremble thinking this dream could
Herald acceptance, if not love
Of my accursed VDL past VDL past,
My daughters leading me like blind
Oedipus to Renison Bell,
Where, inner sight won I'll forgive
The legacy an Empire gave.

(32)

There were no local role models,
No heroes known of as a child,
No Van Diemen's Land Governors I
Could look up to and emulate,
Since Davey was a foul-mouthed thug
Who in public fell drunk off mounts,
Much more at home tossing off rum
With low-lifes than with dignitaries,
Hell's-Gates Sorell an adulterer
Who fathered illegitimates,
Arthur a genocidal cruel
Lipless ramrod-Puritan who
Rubbed sensitive noses like mine
Forever deeper in the dirt.

(33)

Impractical, and labelled as
'A useless arrangement', I was
Born surplus-to-requirements in
A materialistic world of
Sport, two-car families, handymen,
Watching telly ads, mowing lawns,
Putting out, bringing in waste bins,
Gender confusion, lost weekends,
Secretly writing poems in parks,
The albatross Tasman shot in
Discovering the isle slung around
My neck in the form of a birth-
Mark shaped like the triangle to
Which convicts were secured and flogged.

(34)

A hundred inches in a year,
The West Coast's record falls of rain
Meant Pearce-and-Gabbett-haunted swamps,
A clinging sea of mud that bogged
The mine equipment axle-deep
And drove the women to despair,
Especially the house-proud ones
Who couldn't keep the lino clean
Or carpet in the lounge like new,
My cool collected mother thrown,
Provoked to 'bloody', 'bugger', 'damn',
Explosive, scaring rage as she
Cursed weather keeping clothes wet through
For days on lines running with pearls.

(35)

Hospitalised in '63
In Hobart's Royal with alcohol-
Induced pancreatitis, I
Recall its Crimean-War look
Before Florence Nightingale's time,
The Men's Ward like a dormitory
At boarding school with beds that stretched
Endlessly on two sides and made
The aisle a busy road down which
Poisoner-painter Wainewright once wheeled
The corpses while waiting his turn,
Receding in perspective to
The point where a departed soul
Could conceivably merge with God.

(36)

When cancer had Pad by the bowels
And seven years had passed since first
He'd caught my eye and stared me down,
I seized rope thrown, desperate by now
For a guide through my Hell's Gates' maze,
Neglecting Rose to pay him court,
But not before I'd agonised
And put off time and time again
Inviting him to have a drink,
Then calmed by valium approached
And met him next day for lunch in
Hobart's first licensed restaurant,
It being understood at last
That food with booze was for the good.

(37)

A subtle operator, Pad,
By twenty years the older man,
His hand cupped over mine, began
To share his lonely, savage soul,
With weight-loss knee pressed hard as though
He knew in more than earthly ways.
A magic, sure-fire transfer point
Whereby to give me poetry,
His legacy he hoped that like
A relay runner I'd secure,
Giving me an identity
Strong enough to incorporate
My Hell's Gates' convict origins
And soar beyond to love-lit days.

(38)

O Paddy, Paddy, who replaced
The brother I lost as a child
Because of bouts of jealous rage
Parental stupidity caused,
I also cast you in roles such
As Gilgamesh to Enkidu,
Achilles to Patroclus, pairs
Representing idealised love,
Imagined by me out of grief
When you died, aged just fifty-nine,
Burnt-out by sheer intensity
In service as a Cold War Knight,
And to poetry, leaving me
To soldier on companionless.

(39)

'One yearns for Paradise on earth,
But nothing's ever good enough
And always falls short by a mile,
The real world smelly as a fart
Or miners' snuffed-out carbide lamps
Compared with our imaginings,
The Parthenon near-perfect till
The gun-powder stored there blew up,'
Wrote 'A' in eighteen twenty-eight.
Now cars corrode and tourists move
Like maggots on an upside down
Shorn sheep with stone-stiff, stumpy legs,
Its vanished sculptures eyes picked out
By titled English predators.

(40)

'I hope to write an epic poem
Structured like Dante's', 'A' declared,
'Van Diemen's Land with convicts, blacks
The denizens tormented by
Colonial officers in Hell,
With Purgatory the long voyage back
To civilisation, released
From sufferings of the damned, but still
Enduring spiritual malaise
Till the return to cultural bliss,
The Paradise of music, art
In Europe is achieved, its loss
An imperious punishment
Too incalculable for words'.

(41)

If Pad was Dad then Mum was Madge
Ripper, his rival as a bard,
A scintillatingly brilliant,
Highly dangerous bag of tricks
In the interests of furthering her
Stature, buttering me up to be,
As she mischievously put it,
'The meat in our family sandwich',
Lending books, literary magazines,
Typing my poems, giving food
Capriciously mixed in with such
Disturbing innuendoes that
I'd leave with 'box of goodies' half
Mad wondering what she really meant.

(42)

Paddy, perhaps to get me off
His hands, introduced me to Madge
With 'he's a Vandemonian,
A monstrous product of the isle,
As cunning as a shithouse rat,
According to what I've learnt in
His drunken, rambling hearts-to-hearts,
Who gives priority to poems
No matter that they wound, would cut
His granny's throat to publish one,
Is anxious to learn at our feet,
Bend low and kiss them if it adds
A dimension to his lone soul
Conceived between our off-white sheets'.

(43)

Apart from a privileged few free
Settlers, Van Diemen's Land was just
An island given over to
Concentrated convictism,
Where cat-o'-nine tail floggings were
The stock-in-trade punishment to
Such an extent that they've seeped in
To my consciousness till I see
The colony's quintessence as
A stretched tight livid itchy scar
That always when my biro's tip
Scratches it open shows the same
Abyss of horror of backs flayed,
Of torn skin that never quite heals.

(44)

As Mephistopheles, Pad in
Exchange for my allegiance took
Me on as an apprentice bard,
For five years led, as cancer crept
And ate him down to four stone four,
Me in a dance round Hobart Town,
Enthralling with perilous pranks
That added a dimension to
My limited Tasmanian self,
Sexual transferences that
With a deft touch and knowing smile
He'd impishly set up with red-
And dark-haired females till he'd wrecked
All marriages except his own.

(45)

Colon-cankered Pad, keen to star
As two-thirds god Gilgamesh, sent
Courtesan, red-haired Tessy Dawn
To lie with me while Rose was ill
In London showing off our first,
To civilise, bring me in from
The Hell's Gates' West Coast wilderness
As bosom-friend Enkidu, tamed
And groomed for life at his last court,
For talk of matters of the soul,
It all going to my disturbed
VDL/Tassie head that thought
I was now writing poems as good
As bleak bowel-shadowed days allowed.

(46)

The usual dangerous Greek town,
Hania's cracked pavements trip me up
And let me in and out of Hades
Where I've consigned foes still alive
To writhe, where Paddy guiding wipes
His brow, declaring it was much
Hotter for him above! Then I,
Recalling Dido's snubbing of
Aeneas reverse roles and look
An inch above the heads of my
Two divorced English wives as they
Attempt to greet, both of whom I
Rescued from ill-health, one insane,
The other just able to breathe.

(47)

The love I was unable to
Transfer to father, mother, I
Hoarded and gave at thirty-one
As a disturbed lost soul to Pad
And Madge, who by rare good chance lived
In Hobart when I needed them,
Two mainland bards worthy of my
Adulation as opposed to
Any VDL-formed folk I'd
As yet to meet, who failed, unlike
These high-flying newcomers to
Recognise the embryo of
A poet in me, being more
Inclined to shit on such a dream.

(48)

I gave Pad on request my own
Loved annotated copy of
'The Gilgamesh Epic' and he
Kept it, perhaps because he'd seen
Its possibilities for us,
With him as Gilgamesh and I
As Enkidu till Death reversed
The roles, while red-haired Tessy Dawn
Was both the harlot who'd lured me
As wild West Coaster to the Court
Held in various Hobart haunts,
And Siduri, divine barmaid,
With Madge, capricious in real life,
Fickle Ishtar, goddess of love.

(49)

For supernumeraries we drew
On VDL/Tassie's scarce stock
Of talented, beautiful girls
Who didn't measure men's worth by
Possession of goods, but their skills
In bringing richer worlds to light,
Sympatico wenches who poured
The wine at lunches, soirées, to
Lubricate, sanction our quest for
Immortality in poems,
While Pad's mistress, dark-haired, half-caste
Arachne Webb was Death, and at
His real-life one in hospital
Sat with him in a farewell tryst.

(50)

I slowly was confirmed in my
Rich Fate to be a poet by
The red-haired lush, Tessy Dawn, who,
Convict descended like myself
Was a discerning critic of
My monster-slaying early verse,
The ogre Humbaba dispatched
With Pad as Gilgamesh a stand-
In for my West Coast childhood's beasts,
And if he liked one of these poems
He'd publish it in 'Quadrant' as
'Promising apprenticeship stuff',
Persuading me I'd searched and found
The faint beginnings of a voice.

(51)

Between my life in Hobart Town
And the archaic epic's themes,
Parallels abounded, not just
On the level of monsters to
Be slain in quest of poems and fame,
But love and vengeance echoed too,
As Ishtar's overtures spurned by
Gilgamesh doubled in the crush
Madge had on Pad, sending him verse
For publication only to
Receive it back by return post,
Resulting in her boundless rage
Poisoning me as the meat in their
Sandwich when she next took a bite.

(52)

As Ishtar, her love scorned, dispatched
The Bull of Heaven to destroy
The city ruled by Gilgamesh,
So Madge failing in her feud with
Pad to turn me against him, which,
As I've said, poisoned me as meat,
Began to woo my wife Eve in
Preference to me, and even more
Wounding sabotaged a book of
Poetry we were billed to share,
Making sure it never appeared,
Reasons, that added to all those
For leaving VDL/Tas weighed
Most heavily in my resolve.

(53)

'Great poet, shit of a female',
In my rare case Madge Ripper was
A loving kind generous friend till
Her ambition to be hailed best
Unleashed paranoid jealousy
To the point of insanity,
And so her eyes cut off my head
As too close to her rival Pad,
As possible threat to her rise,
Breeding mistrust till our friendship
Thinned to exchanging Christmas Cards,
Her Wittgenstein-like spouse who thought
Versifiers enemies of
Philosophy also estranged.

(54)

Untrustworthy, vindictive as
Ishtar smirking as she vowed in
'The Epic of Gilgamesh to
Never unleash The Flood again,
Madge, mother's milk curdled, loaned me
The family dinghy to fish from,
Letting me know that I was now
Living dangerously, a row-
Lock all but eaten through with rust
Snapping, forcing me, no seaman,
To improvise with worn-thin belt,
Strap oar in place and near-undone
By panic mixed with rage head home
Hoping fickle Poseidon slept.

(55)

The closest that I got to Pad
Was by sharing in his last days,
Then inheriting, his mistress,
Named 'Arachne' by me because
Bobby-pins strewn around her bed
Made it a trapdoor's web, though she
As death-goddess Irkalla in
Our enacted epic helped him,
Gilgamesh-become-Enkidu,
To die in a state of near bliss,
But for me, as new hero-king,
Was anathema, and one more
Reason, her drinking luring me,
Now teetotal, for leaving Tas.

(56)

Death rubbing my nose in its dark
Business, I wept for Enkidu,
Worms beginning to drop from his,
Then set out on my quest alone
To never suffer his gross Fate,
Darkness not lifting till I met
Red-haired Tessy Dawn as divine
Barmaid Siduri tempting with:
'Only family can comfort man',
But reading my need as profound
At last pointed the way to where
Utnapishtim forever lives,
In Hania with a climate that
Knows not Tasmania's withering cold.

(57)

The Cretan Elders in all shapes,
In baggy jodhpurs and high boots,
Their leathery faces seamed like Pad's,
Move with the dignity and grace
Of Jurassic Park animals,
Disagree on the rights and wrongs
Of Greece's lively politics,
Shout, wave arms about, then still smile
Though nothing's solved, as daintily
They sip, treat ouzo with respect,
Greet, farewell with a kiss, give flowers,
Compared to booze-mad Tassie brutes
As ill-dressed as emus, gum-trees,
Sentenced by history to defeat.

Block Three

(1)

Hania Park's mellow light's a balm
After the harsh corroding skin
Cancer-giving Tasmanian sun,
While linden, oak, birch, elm, ash, beech,
Pine, cypress, deodar are spaced
At intervals that please the eye,
As are the walkways fanning out,
Where in the silence one might hear
God's 'here I am' as Adam did,
Meet Eve, innocent, dressed for love
In the perfection of her flesh,
Not Gabbett dribbling blood as he,
Rain-forest drenched, goes slouching through
The chaos of dense undergrowth.

(2)

Vulnerably wide-open for signs
To mean what I would like them to,
The furiously fluttering wings
Of startled doves massage my heart
Skipping beats in wonder that such
Powerfully symbolic birds would send
A message through my blood that I've
Been chosen by The Holy Ghost
To sit in Hania's park and write
An epic poem in praise of God,
And when their wing-tips graze my head,
Disturb the surface of my skin,
Soul in its thick-walled cell could be
About to fly free of despair.

(3)

My student years spent rotten drunk
In homage to my troubled self,
Bar-room life in Hobart demeaned
As when not throwing up we skulled
And indecipherably snarled
A greeting to a mate and picked
Noses, nags from 'The Mercury',
Told jokes about the dirty cunt
Who'd shoved his cock up some bloke's arse,
An 'Aloyishus' poem blunt:
'The convivial English pub
With fireside, food, mixed company
Was in Van Diemen's Land turned by
Despair into a swillery'.

(4)

As Gilgamesh after Pad's death,
I'd crossed Death's Waters to Crete, met
Immortal Utnapishtim as
An Elder who tested to see
If I was worthy of his state,
Could withstand sleep as on he droned,
And failing woke to flowers, which worn
As a consoling second prize
Rejuvenated, yet drove me
To indulge in skinfuls, espy
A petalled snake sloughing as it
Slid off, but not to slip back in
To alcoholism, poems now
My way to win undying fame.

(5)

A few months before Paddy passed,
Writing faith-wavering poems to start
Him on his journey home to God,
Or else snuffed out at once he'd stay
Eternally dead in the dark,
He let me read some sonnets called
'Gilgamesh Laments His Loss', then
Tantalisingly withdrew them,
But implying I follow on
With what I could recall: 'the dream
Was wondrous, the terror great, we
Must cherish it, not count the cost
Of marriages and children lost,
Careers abandoned for its sake!'

(6)

I walked up Ocean Beach with Rose
To breathe and sense the atmosphere
Of the infamous Hell's Gates' gaol
And lost her in a Thames-thick fog
That crept about us as she moaned
And shuddered in the wicked cold,
The she-oaks dripping as it swirled
In shapes that filled her with unease
And drove Tassie's past like a wedge
Between us all day there and back,
The sea a hidden, muffled beast
With 'Aloyishus' whispering:
'Transported for the love of one,
An English Rose must bleed for me'.

(7)

With an expert on 'For The Term
Of His Natural Life' in tow, Rose
And I, giving each other hell,
Drove each day from Strahan as our base
To Rosebery, Zeehan, Queenstown whose stump-
Pocked sulphur-eaten slopes streamed with
Rusty water, as though Old Nick
Drying-out with DTs, the shakes,
Had made a mess trying to shave,
To 'Gormy', where Hell's red primrose
Around the gravelled sport's ground brought
Back memories of skun bleeding knees,
Brutes toppling me for fancy ways,
Though I still kicked the winning goal!

(8)

The Marcus Clarke scholar upset
By the raw-meat look of the West
Was bad enough to contend with,
But Rose, critical of the place,
And quite unable to believe
I grew up there, destroyed my cool,
Reality deserting her
Abortion-addled mind as I,
Drawing on loyalties thought long dead
Defended, outraged when she did
A poo in cannibalised scrub
And didn't cover it with leaves,
Feared fantasies of murdering her
Further scrambling my haunted head.

(9)

Though I in line with Mother's wrath
Could judge the remote West Coast as
'Not fit for human consumption',
I leapt to its defence when out-
Siders like pommy Rose scorned it,
The ghost of 'Aloyishus' keen
To have her throttled then and there
For high falutin' ways with rough-
And-ready chip-on-shoulder folk,
Her Oxbridge accent, withering looks
Offensive in crude spit-slimed bars
Where wheezy old timers, young slobs,
Begrimed bowyanged miners still cringed
Beneath race memories of the lash.

(10)

'The Stain' still stunts my VDL-
Dwarfed soul as I search through its mess,
My hatred of poms that sent kin
As far away as possible,
Greedy imperialists intent
On grabbing distant, world's-end lands,
The class divorced mad Rose sums up
When arrogantly she demands
More money yet to feed 'my girls'
Despite her wealth, manor in Bath,
A house in London rented to
Colonials paying through the nose,
Obsequious pilgrims who peep
Through bars for glimpses of the Queen.

(11)

'I wanted an Australian stud,
A six-foot wild colonial boy
To sire my children and make good
Two I aborted in the back
Streets of Paris aged seventeen,
Not some weak-chested English runt
Diseased by lack of sun and food,
But one, mission achieved, to be
Again dumped on 'The Fatal Shore',
Since how could such an upstart with
An ugly accent help to bring
My girls up once we'd returned Home,
How introduce him to my friends?',
Was no doubt Rose thinking aloud.

(12)

'You bastard!', shrilled the broken Rose,
Then Eve, also depressed by me
Who'd made them suffer badly for
The Empire's crimes, especially its
Creation of my troubled self,
Seemingly born to misery,
But getting their own back now as,
Show-jumpers both, haughtily they
Rode me past England's winning post,
Leaving me stranded in the field,
Humiliatingly spent as
Cruelly they galloped on and on
With knowing smile, then lay fulfilled,
Expectant of a cup of tea.

(13)

Enamoured of Thomas Hobb's 'Life
Is nasty, brutal and short-lived',
My Pearce-Gabbett strain takes the form
Of savouring blood when brushing my
Alcohol-caused, scurvy-soft gums,
Of fearing I'll hang myself, since
Dropping off to sleep's like I've plunged
Through a trapdoor beneath my feet,
Rope playing out, jerking me wide
Awake to sit bolt upright, test
My map-of-Tassie birthmarked neck
I've so far found too thick to fit
The knot beneath my ear, evolved
To outwit Jack Ketch at his best.

(14)

At Rosebery, home until ten
Within the shadow of Mount Black
That leans out from the top and falls
Forever on the mining town,
We stopped for lunch, Rose shaken by
The varicose-veined redneck girls
With booze and pasties on their breath
Walking in slippers down the street,
My guilt flashing with 'I'd no right
To transplant her to backward Tas
To view worst features, my love-hate
Feelings for poms who made it so
Rendering me unable to help
Her struggling hard to settle in'.

(15)

Brakes failing as we left the West,
Rose broken by the trip behind
The wheel as we discussed our plight,
Gears slowing us to a crawl, it
Seemed cowardly when the expert on
'For The Term Of His Natural Life'
Leapt from the car, an insult to
The characters on whom he wrote,
Who gave him a well-paid career
But endured so much more than him,
This soft fleshy academic,
'Herg',with barely decipherable
Whining adenoidal drawl, as
If always depressed about life.

(16)

'Ours, all ours!', screeched the demons of
Van Diemen's Land, fighting among
Themselves to seize the branding iron,
Apply it sizzling to my neck
And leave Tasmania mapped out there.
'This will ensure that driven to
Break all the rules governing life here
From tyrannical Arthur's time
He'll double down to leave no doubt,
Throw lawfulness to the winds, leave
Wife, daughters, jobs, ignore contracts,
Become a drunkard, womanise,
Just to show he hadn't been cowed!',
They caterwauled in unison.

(17)

At Rosebery I'd shown Rose,
Parting a way through blackberries,
Where once the Picture Theatre stood,
Remembering how I'd break my neck
Twisting round in my seat to spot
My mother in her good brown coat,
Boronia in the buttonhole,
Raised on a ramp with Peggy Burns,
The Super's wife, anxious to move
From pick-and-shovel class to Staff,
Pitch darkness now the film I saw,
Feeling I lived in No Man's Land,
Disoriented, dispossessed,
At home nowhere in all the world.

(18)

A ghost town, Renison Bell's mill
Was just fire-blackened beams and ribs
Exposed to Rose's drug-dulled eyes,
The railway station boarded up
Because Garret and Goods trains no
Longer passed through like hells on wheels
As lonely I'd watched out for them,
Feeling forgotten, left to die
Amongst the washing always wet
On our verandah out the front,
The water race across the line
That fed flotation tables to
Further process the low grade tin
Now as dry as my arid soul.

(19)

These days my VDL past's rope
That hangs me from Crete's olive trees,
Heat-hazed asphalt roads swirling with
Mirages of menacing blacks,
Railways in Athens alive with
West Coast fettlers in blueys soaked
With rain and sweated rot-gut grog,
Sea bringing in Hell's Gates' dregs to
Make where I'm living just a dump,
While Greece corrupted, brought low by
Rats in high office stripping it,
Is a rabid dog threatening to
Hunt me down in streets choked with un-
Emptied bins and Tas images.

(20)

In Zeehan where Dame Melba sang,
The Gaiety Theatre's walls reeked from
Damp pale grey fungal growths lit by
Flickering lights, flames through which forebear
'Aloyishus Featherstone' spoke
As Prometheus chained to near-
By Trial Harbour volcanic rock,
The relentlessly nibbling gulls
Tormenting him to burst out with:
'The fire I gave to you will die
Unless you write an epic poem
Redeeming life in this foul hole',
Rose sobbing, looking on as I
Scribbled another sonnet down.

(21)

In honour of Tasmania's past,
The West Coast as a horror film
Showed on The Gaiety's rotting walls:
Pearce axing, wolfing mates'meat, while,
Yellowed hair rolled in old newsprint,
Folk smoked it for the nicotine,
Old-lag labourers coughing black blood,
'Truth's' photos of the chained child starved
To death by parents on Mount Black
Pricking our Rosebery consciences,
As was Renison's, its Bell rung
For the mine horse of that name Des
Finn beat to death with a crowbar
For failing to pull trucks through mud.

(22)

Also screening as I toured with
Rose wilting was myself, a child
Running around our rubbish bin,
My bête noir 'Boofhead' in pursuit,
As though it was the walls of Troy
And I Hector who'd cut and run
From Achilles hot on my heels,
Mother shouting from a top step,
Arms akimbo, to stand and fight
Him like a man, who now unnerved,
Hungover, hallucinating,
Sucked up his Fate to have a wife
As throwback to her, quite without
Emotional means to support.

(23)

This film was then supplanted by
My brother on a swing I pushed
Up rafter-high until he jumped,
Fell flat upon his face and blocked
Tear ducts for life, none of the probes,
For which chloroform made him sick,
Doing the job in Launceston
A day's bus ride from where we lived
At Rosebery in the West, so that
We had to stay with relatives
A few miles out, the 'accident'
Giving him buck-teeth too, four knocked
Into teaseable prominence,
So scant my empathy for him.

(24)

Film festival arising out
Of childhood trauma ended with
A major row with Rose who screamed
She couldn't stand the ugliness
And had to return 'Home' at once,
To her own horror show in which
Abortion is the villain I
Thought as we left the rotting hall,
Just after I'd seen yet again
My younger brother's brow gashed as
I seized our shared pick in rage, then
Dug holes to bury him, mum, dad,
Who terminating love for me
Lavished it on his ravenous heart.

(25)

As Homer's epic catalogued
Ships, cities, warriors involved
In war for faithless Helen's sake,
I've listed West Coast horror shows
Experienced as a child and now
Lived with as veterans do their hell,
Since violence, ugliness endure
As trauma lurking, threatening all
One's life to dismantle the mind,
Disturbing in strange, subtle ways,
Some wounds less obvious, disguised,
Discomfiting with vague unease
Beyond the scope of therapy,
Loving kindness, or God to cure.

(26)

Evelyn Helen Wintergate:
I married her to live the myths
Encapsulated in her name,
The sex and treachery evoked,
For something cool and abstract in
Her surface that disguised the rage
The mutilating doctors left,
Her sheer pretence that made it hard
To pick the evil twist below
Her icily presented show,
The bitterness from being one
Lung short, aware as Paris that
She'd dump me in the end for theft
From Menelaus whom she loved.

(27)

The wall had also flickered with
My father falling from the back
Of a ute delivering him drunk
From golf one Sunday night, with me
Rushing to help him up, lead to
The woodshed where he sobbed about
Not daring to venture inside
As his cold wife, my mother, tried
To overcome my sister's wrath
From feeding on breasts running dry,
My arm around him as he perked
In chips we carefully picked to heat
Bathroom water, and my cat to
Fastidiously cover poo.

(28)

My father, though, was disloyal in
His siding with my English wife,
Given to schadenfreude, as when,
Without phoning he just dropped in
One Monday morning on Rose ill
And barely managing the kids,
On me hungover from a lost
Weekend and having hairs of dogs
Before I could prepare for that
Day's lectures and tutorials,
And he instead of joining me
In sympathy had tea with her,
Excusing himself with 'a bit
Early' and enjoying my shame.

(29)

The joylessness, sheer lack of fun
In Rosebery, Zeehan, Renison Bell,
My parents' lack of empathy
For silicotic pensioners
Habitually dead-drunk and gaoled,
Not just by cops, but life itself,
Their claustrophobic dread of bush
Always needing to be cut back,
Apprehension of Nature as
Snakes, blowies, slugs, jack-jumpers' nests,
The run-down houses with cheap light-
Weight sticks of unmatched furniture
Making them more like camps than homes,
All gave the West its ambience.

(30)

Door locked, Maple's suite under wraps,
We hardly used the sitting room,
Save for 'rellies' on Boxing Day,
Its chilling emptiness replaced
By good-suited formality
When it became 'The Lounge', fireplace
Obsessively ochred by my
Mother with little else to do,
While during farewells till this time
Next year, my brother and I climbed,
Truce called, onto the couch and squashed
Heat-drugged blowies against a pane,
Fingerprints, maggots left in dust
Crime punishable with a belt.

(31)

I've never known why, when home
During boarding school vacations,
Aged twelve to seventeen, depressed,
At Renison Bell in the West
Where human debris had washed up,
I lived consumed by morbid dread
That vigilance required to guard
Against committing the worst crime
Imaginable would fail me,
And suddenly, blacked out, I'd kill
My ten years younger sister. Was
It out of loneliness, need to
Identify, belong among
Tasmania's lowest of the low?

(32)

Or was my phobia to be
Explained by jealousy of her
Because I'd not been born the girl
Peers saw me as, or did her birth
Deeply disturb since it meant loss
Of even more interest in me
First suffered on my sixteen months
Younger brother's advent, or was
It, fathomlessly complex, caused,
Given my maddening love of her,
By unconscious fear of incest,
Deep-rooted in a district where
Large isolated families could
Live seven to a water tank?

(33)

Moonlight flooding our shared bedroom,
I'd keep myself awake for fear
I might sleepwalk and kill her as
She lay tucked up, my sister loved
Obsessively by me, outraged
Because my parents wouldn't let
Me pet her as much as I wished,
Tales of incest in Tassie's back-
Ward West no doubt conditioning them.
And if my knight-like vigil failed
I'd wake in panic, cross the floor,
Kneel down, relieved to know she breathed,
Hair not bloodied, but golden as
An angel's in a picture book.

(34)

The railway cuttings narrow, dark,
My wet hand holding hers, we'd walk
Through them to Bowen's Dump for milk,
Afraid I'd push her underneath
The Goods or Garrett roaring by
As we stood pinned against wet rock
As flat as we could make ourselves.
I'd grab her when they'd passed and throw
Her wildly up and down for joy,
Bring her to rest and kiss my tears
Blinking gem-like upon her cheeks,
The bridge that without railings spanned
A long drop to a mine-fouled stream
The next hazard looming ahead.

(35)

Another drunken row with Rose,
Next day, despite my vow to end
Self-indulgence, the wall revealed
An angry Rosebery bathroom scene,
My mother roughly towelling what
She dismissed as a water tap,
Resisting my attempts to hug
And kiss her as she knelt to clothe
Me in a lace-edged vest to go
With bonnet-shaped headdress, cape, case,
Provoking boys in caps, raincoats
With bags strapped to backs, arms, legs free
To bash, kick IT she'd also called
Mouse, peanut, witchetty grub, snake.

(36)

I love the anonymity
An Islamised, debased Greece gives,
Where my nicknames, 'Cissy', 'Blossom', won't
Be shouted at me in the street,
Or chance encounters trigger shame-
Ful memories of fifteen years spent
In Hobart bars, my failure to
Come to terms with Van Diemen's Land,
The texture of daily life that
Aroused the hackles of my soul
And made me much prefer the loud-
Mouthed, awesomely-arsed Hellenes, plague
Of smoking vehicles, the fact
That most of them are really Turks.

(37)

As Philip Larkin understood,
'They fuck you up, your mum and dad,
They may not mean to, but they do',
As force-fed kids in Greece reveal,
Sucking on sweetened teats from birth
Till nine or ten, making of them
The future monsters who'll indulge
Base appetites life-long, replace
Merely themselves as rumours grow
Of womanising, greed, then spread
In turn the lie that history will
Not be repeated under them,
Until they're booted out to watch
Replicas do more of the same.

(38)

Manic 'Cassandra' absent from
Hania's park leaves me only free
To think about Van Diemen's Land,
Dwell on Piranesi's prints, their
Innumerable cages, cells
Still housing all the devils of
My Tassie mind, despite my dis-
Charge to live at large writing poems,
In search of God-alone-knows-what.
I find I miss her though, the wild
Prophecies that I will, my two
Daughters sacrificed, soon fall in
To some fierce, outrageously wronged,
Revengeful Clytemnestra's hands.

(39)

My race memory in overdrive,
I loathed on sight 'Tadpole' Sorell,
Spawn of the Hell's Gates founder who'd
Brought convicts' hero Mike Howe low.
My boarding school housemaster, he'd
Nicknamed me 'Blossom', hung it round
My adolescent neck and called
Me 'Billy Budd' from time to time,
Said, despite my origins, I
Showed promise, and that under him,
Taught better table manners than
Gabbett or Pearce, should do quite well,
The same who'd whipped my buttocks raw,
Bequeathed a victim's cast of mind.

(40)

A Cain who slew his sister too,
If only in the mind, I sent,
Instinctively, myself to gaol,
Withdrawing from life out of shame,
That built into a phobia
That I might run amuck and kill,
Since people were the enemy
Who'd doomed me to become a Jack
The Ripper, Christie, John George Haigh,
The latter's vampire cravings read
About in a wind-blown 'Truth'
Found when I chased a cricket ball
Like a red hunk of meat into
Tussocks round Zeehan's school playground.

(41)

My brother chloroformed ten times
To try and probe his tear duct clear
Meant ten walks round the Albert Park
In Launceston to bring him to,
And ten trips with him vomiting
On the bus back to Cressy where
On the tenth of September I
Had my tenth birthday, father at
Rosebery working in the mine,
Complaining that he couldn't pay
The doctor's bill or Uncle Sam
For having us to stay ten weeks
For less than guest house rates, the eye
Watering to this day from my crime.

(42)

In our school Social Studies' book
Called 'Out Of The Mist', to which we
Added 'And Into The Fog', there
Was scant mention of convicts, blacks,
As though there were no shadows in
Tasmania's white settlement past,
And that it was a case of 'all
Things bright and beautiful', of life
'On the sunny side of the street',
Of 'rule Britannia, rule the waves',
And not till Uni days when I
Formed friendships with historians
Like Robson Reynolds McCrae Roe
Did anything like 'truth' prevail.

(43)

At least the swarthy offspring of
Governor Sorell's adulterous days
In the West Indies matched his new
Van Diemen's Land environment,
The fur of devils, skins of blacks,
Seals, whales, the shadows sweeping hills,
Mount Wellington relentlessly,
As though trying to unearth some-
Thing even darker underneath,
A background at odds with blush-red,
Tripe-white poms looking imposed on
Yet obtruding from landscapes formed
Beneath a sun hostile to their
Insipid, pallid presences.

(44)

Lone wolf with no allegiances,
The thylacine's my familiar,
No expert able yet to prove
If it's extinct, or hides away,
Imprisoned by suspiciousness
Acquired sensing the fate of blacks,
Their disappearance overnight,
Relatively speaking, because,
Child-like, they'd trusted Robinson
And Truganini, followed them,
Persuaded life would be improved.
Therefore it's chosen to hole up
In corners too remote for men,
Or flee transmogrified to Crete.

(45)

At Trial Harbour Rose confused
Me with the English cad who'd de-
Flowered but made her bud, hang head
In shame and to twice terminate
Much wanted pregnancies, then with
Her father who'd died just before
We met, but like me had grey hair,
A first in Classics, love of verse
And alcohol, neglecting her,
The last of three, as he declined,
As I, with her newly arrived,
Touring the isle grew more obsessed
With relating its past to me
Than helping her acclimatise.

(46)

A poet manqué serving time
In publishing, her father was
An emphysemic, chauffeured drunk,
The muse inspiring not his work,
But him to fund John Betjeman.
He married corgi-petting Dot,
A twin-set, blue-rinse idiot
And bridge fanatic without skill,
Both spoiling Rose rotten with cash
As a solution to her ills,
As he sat self-absorbed and failed
To jog her like the others on
His knee, fell backwards down the stairs
Cradling a bottle in his arms.

(47)

Waves nightmarishly high at Trial
Harbour, where Tasman, driven by
The Roaring Forties couldn't land,
Rose, to be heard above two gales,
The strongest blowing in her head,
Screamed out denunciations of,
Not just the cad, her father, me,
But of her London shrink she'd kept
Me from, because he'd wished, now we
Were to marry and live in Tas,
To warn me that her depressed state
Might sometimes release itself in
Dangerous psychotic episodes,
Pushing me cliff-wards as she raged.

(48)

My father wouldn't risk his Chev
Upon the pot-holed road to Trial,
But once I went with Ned and Floyd
Bowen from Renison Bell, rode
The rust-holed tray of their old wreck
To where huge blue sea, matching sky
Had left room for a few crude tin
And weatherboard shacks knocked up by
West Coast miners for weekend jags,
For blowies with dull yellow tails
That stormed the smelly crayfish shells
Thrown with the empties out the back,
Six foot tiger snakes basking on
The basalt rocks as we arrived.

(49)

Mine foreman, Ned cracked snakes like whips,
Had hernias the size of fists
From lifting trucks back onto lines
He'd laid and cut the sleepers for,
Clamped detonators with loose chipped
Inherited false teeth to fuse
Cut short to save a bob, lost bits
of fingers to adzes when he
In hobnail boots slipped barking gums
For Bell the mare and I who could
Misdirect with 'gee' for 'wo back',
To deliver to a shack-sized
Railway station mostly used as
A dunny minus seat and can.

(50)

The mine horse Bell bludgeoned to death
By the recidivist Des Finn,
I drove and rode another named
The same, chafed thighs' insides on flanks
As chestnut-hued and steaming-warm
As loaves of bread Ned's missus baked,
Had 'Floydy-love', their son, the Seth
And Elvis of the West, as friend,
Who showed respect when I observed
That possums' noses glowed as if
They smoked, that trout we stunned with guns
Had spots just like my father's coat,
An image I felt worried by
Each time I saw him wearing it.

(51)

As Achille's horses declared,
If it wasn't Nestor or Thetis,
That he must bravely choose between
A packed hour of fame-winning life
Or longer one without a name,
So I imagine mine horse Bell
Whispered that I could remain safe
Sulking in Tas or strike out for
Adventures in the cities of
Europe, fulfilling myself by
Writing immortal poetry
Inspired by Art and femmes fatales
As dark and elegantly poised
As blackbirds in the winter snow.

(52)

Like Seth in Stella Gibbon's 'Cold
Comfort Farm', Floyd's menacing back-
Wood's, loutish cow-lick, jowly mien,
Elvis Presley pout, drew West Coast
Women ranging from mother who
Confessed he looked a bit like Paul
Newman, to shift workers' wives, girls
Who wore no pants and let you look
For nothing but a twisted neck
Under their helpfully raised desks,
To alcoholic Mrs Ives
He shagged for bottles of bad booze,
At school measuring his horn at six
Inches to show who ruled the roost.

(53)

Where's Dante's ordered universe,
Hierarchical, common-sense world,
The certainty of God's great love,
The natural progression through
A hell and purgatory into
An everlasting paradise?
Where's Homer's strict heroic code
Men died for knowing right from wrong,
Rewards and punishments that gave
Time-sanctioned meaning to a life?
Where's Gilgamesh's homage to
Reality, his walls built with
An apotropaic poem carved
On them to guard the soul as well?

(54)

'Is Neddy Bowen any good?',
I'd ask my father driving to
Zeehan on Friday arvo to
Bring home 'The Roast', to have a few
While I, bored, waited in the car.
'Give him half a chance and he'd shake
The eye out of a needle son.
Too lairy with his bodgie side-
Burns, fruit-salad shirts, for my taste.
Dead loss as foreman of the mine.
Can't keep his distance from the men.
Mind you, his wife has let him down.
A real good sport, but fat as mud
And doesn't keep the house too clean'

(55)

'George Delbridge seems a nice old man'.
'Alright. Been single all his life.
Appears to like the ladies though.
Strange sort of bird to end up here
As metallurgist at the mill.
It beats me what he does weekends.
He doesn't punt the gee-gees much.
Two bob each way's about his lot.
I reckon his de facto's cut
Her fingers pulling purse strings tight.
I have to check his assaying.
Too many blues to be much help.
These Uni blokes aren't practical.
Their theories only work in books'.

(56)

'Fred Berry doesn't seem much good'.
'No-hoper, son. Those jags of his
Will end him up in Lachlan Park.
He played footy for Rosebery
As full forward, and I've seen him
Turn on threepence, sneak goals between
The posts as close as prison bars.
His people weren't much chop, they'd all
Have swung till not so long ago.
Great miner though, goes at it like
The grog's a shovelful away,
Then enough earnt to wipe the slate
Clean from last time and do it all
Over again he disappears!'

(57)

'What's Tommy Clarke like underground?'
'Champion when he's off the grog.
The only skilled man on the job,
He trucks out more ore in a day
Than all the others in a week
For screw higher than even mine.
You couldn't fit a coffin in
The ratholes where he'll lie to drill
And lay his charges for the quartz
In seams thinner than a whipsnake.
His missus dresses well. Quiet sort.
She'd get on with your Mum, but he's
The Union Rep, a stirrer I'm
Sick to death of having blues with!'

(58)

'Is 'Dunny Can' happier now
He's shacked up with Ma Edgerton?'
'He's Mr Wilkinson to you!
Dunbar passes me on the line
Without bothering to say 'g'day'.
The trouble is he was the boss
When I was just the billy boy.
And now I'm manager he hates
As foreman of the Mill my raids
To catch who's sleeping on their shift.
He's got a hernia too big
For our wheelbarrow, and his de
Facto's bad tucker doesn't help
To put him in a better mood!'

(59)

'Is Alby Webster a good bloke?'
'No! He beats his wife black and blue
And half his wage is garnisheed
To pay for booze ticked up the year
He went on a jag with the town
Bike Mrs 'Burl' Ives then shot through.
I gave him the bullet when he chucked
Fuses, fracture down a shaft, since
I'd clipped him hard under the ear
For giving me a bit of lip.
I've put him on again and hope
The cheeky bugger's learnt some sense.
No wonder Renison Bell Mine
Can't earn shareholders dividends!'

(60)

And what about Mr Howard?'
'He's not the full pack of cards, son.
The way he drives that Plymouth round
You'd think no one else had a car.
As 'Mayor' of Zeehan and owner of
Its hardware store and timber mill,
With other string pullers, all crooks,
He got away with cutting down
King Billy pine to build a yacht
For Tommy Dalton, minister
Of Lands and Works and on the take.
They're RCs and not fit to trust,
Who donate big time to the Church
To get a spot in Paradise'.

(61)

Clean-mouthed, he might continue with:
'As cunning as a you-know-what
And tighter than a fish's bum,
The 'Mayor' didn't shout the bar when
He was acquitted because Miss
Dunkley not only burnt the books
But office down to be quite sure.
He did dig deep though to reward
With house, car, Gold Coast holidays
For sticking her neck out so far.
But he's a bad 'un. Can't keep still.
His eczema, nervous twitch add to
His general shiftiness, drive him
To drink top shelf instead of beer.'

(62)

A caterpillar on a branch,
The old green schoolbus crept along
The thirteen miles of hilly road,
While on the spare tyres in the boot
Floyd shagged the witless Myrtle Dunn.
I sat against doors to stop drunks
Getting out as we crawled homewards,
Between Jack Grubb and the pane that
He smashed to get a sky-filled glass,
Spilling his wasted self on me,
Nursed plonk-filled hessian sugar sacks
That smelt of fly-blown meat and dogs,
Dreaming at nights I was a dark
Red butterfly that flew away.

Block Four

(1)

Outside Hobart's gaol convicts swing
From scaffolding erected for
Their public execution, dance,
As they have never done before,
Variations on Irish jigs
They sadly have no partner for
Though they are eight all in a row,
Each taken up with last thoughts they'll
Share only with Old Nick, as I
Snap to from this nightmare as both
Judge and hangman, black beanie still
In place to keep out winter's cold
Resembling their head-dress worn to
Enact their roles in this ritual.

(2)

I wake and find in sheer relief
I haven't murdered anyone —
Lord, keep it that way till the end –
And lie luxuriating in
The knowledge that it was a dream .
Lord, please always confine me so.
I take deep breaths, reprieved again
From walking in my sleep to kill -
Controls relaxed, restraints removed -
My sister in obedience to
'Each man kills the thing he loves', Wilde's
Aphorism pinpointing our
Weakness for mad, irrational acts.
Lord, double guards against this Fate!

(3)

My dad opined his brother Ron
Suffered because folk judged he'd wed
'Beneath himself', my mum her as
His 'lesser half', a 'trollop' for
Sitting with legs apart out on
The front steps as she boozed and threw
Empties into the scrub, still in
Slippers and dressing gown she'd hitch
Up high to warm her legs before
A radiator that left them
Reticulated with red lines,
For dropping aitches in a drawl
Claimed as incomprehensible
To superior Kiwi ears.

(4)

My snow-queen snobbish mother banned
Me from going to play at fat
Sensual Aunty Aileen's place
Because she gave me smelly hugs
And had a swarm of dirty kids,
'Breeds like a rabbit' a cliche
I learned from talk condemning her,
One of whom was a spastic, I
Mucked round with in his cot, helped
To clamber up the rails despite
Strict warnings not to, since if caught
Out aping him when the wind changed
I'd stay trapped like that all my life,
Such was the superstition then.

(5)

The disadvantaged Ian died
At thirteen, mentally aged two,
Was found fallen from his small cot
In which I'd tried to help him stand,
Not knowing that he could escape
A fate of lingering on and on.
And though he was then my one friend
I still had to fight for the right,
Bestowed at the eleventh hour,
To attend the church service, if
Not the graveside, it being thought
Eight was too young for the ordeal,
Confirmed when I went berserk in
A last mad mimicry of him.

(6)

Madge Ripper with the small sharp teeth
Of a piranha shredded me,
And I sentence her, for the time
Being well known for her poems,
Even famous, to fester in
Oblivion, for mimicking
My putting on the dog acquired
From life with Rose and other poms,
For sabotaging a book we
Were meant to share, putting it round
She much preferred to fly alone
Than with me whose verse was as dark
And unable to transcend life
As Gabbett gnawing on a bone.

(7)

With Rose unfocussed, in and out,
Abusing me in my four roles
Of father, husband, poet, shrink,
We drove to Ross to see the bridge,
The images the convicts carved
She wouldn't get her feet wet for,
To view the Boyds and Nolans hung
In Hans von Muller's stately home,
Who as a good friend from the past
To the extent of sharing girls,
Had wished to please me and my wife,
Till medication, booze, mood mixed
Decided her to judge his pile
'A colonial imitation'.

(8)

An Aloyishus poem reads:
'As an assigned convict I met
On George Meredith's property
The painter-forger-poisoner
Wainewright sketching a servant-girl,
An evil, queasy-looking wench
Whose tense-faced smirking awfulness
Was there forever to remind
The viewer of lost innocence
In females of a tender age.
Back home I'd seen him happy in
The company of Byron, Keats,
But now among moronic brutes
He wore a twisted Goya smile'.

(9)

In Hobart's Battery Point there lived
In Mona Street grotesques and strains
Peculiar to Van Diemen's Land,
Arachne Webb among them, who
As dying Paddy's goddess of
The nether world in our take on
'The Epic of Gilgamesh', was
To be mine at his death if I,
As her fellow-hater of poms,
Could accept her embittered half-
Caste taunting of Rose so depressed
And wilting she became a stalk,
Leaves, petals stripped, with nowhere left
Beneath which to shelter her head.

(10)

'Spoilt-rotten pommy bitch come here
To rub our noses in the shit',
Tar-brushed Arachne lashed out with,
Shacked up with me while Rose depressed
Was hospitalised, yanking out
From her wardrobe a Harrod's coat
That so maddened her she forgot
The rest and hung it on a knob,
Ripping buttons off as a crow
The eyes from a sheep on its back,
As from folk Arthur swung for fun,
Scattering them over me in bed,
Then swanning round in it before
She lay as Lady Muck to fuck.

(11)

Rose bundled into hospital,
I called police when she, her heart
Rate dangerously high escaped,
Came running drugged through Hobart Town,
Back home lest tough male nurses dragged
Her down the long sad corridors
To take pot luck with ECT.
Returned, she still wouldn't sign forms
Permitting them to 'blast' her mind
So as husband, shrinks pressing me,
Conflicted in my feelings, I
Gave my consent on her behalf,
Pad nodding in agreement when
I told him of my dilemma.

(12)

VDL/Tas was heaven for
Those geniuses', 'eccentrics',
Who for whatever reasons had
Become disenchanted elsewhere,
As was the case with poet Pad,
As well as weirdos, ratbags who'd
Fled to avoid being struck off,
Debarred from practising their tricks,
One of whom was a pom I helped
Coerce my crazed wife into care,
A weird quack finally gaoled for
Killing a girl for the sake of
A heightened sexual ecstasy
By cutting off her oxygen.

(13)

I've never known where I belong,
Since Launceston Church Grammar School
Was home to 'The Establishment's'
Offspring, and I was a ring-in
From the isle's lower-deck West Coast,
Sent to an Eton-styled outfit
To have a better chance in life,
This complicated by the fact
That my loyalties had been formed by
The time I got there and weren't all
Undone by housemaster Sorell,
Kin of a Governor who'd had
Mine flogged, such is the key to my
Peculiar personality.

(14)

Lost island-paradise, I miss
The East Coast's Peron Dunes that stretch
For miles deserted since folk fear
The emptiness of sea and sky
They don't know how to cash in on,
The middens testifying to
The blacks at home in bone-bright sand,
Superior to herds of whites
Penned up in cars, fenced lawns and drives,
Afraid to ever be alone,
Who have no gods of air and light,
Nor can read frescoes that the wind
Carves out and then obliterates
As in the story of our lives.

(15)

The East redeems the scowling West
With sunlit beaches fit for Christ
To walk on risen from the dead,
With wafer-white, transparent shells
Blacks feasting after a hunt left
As part of the natural world
Before poms, complicating, came,
Evolving into bogan-styled
Genetically under-privileged
Tasmanians on motor-bikes that
Like enemy attacks erupt,
Rip fragile harmony to bits
With no regard shown for rare souls
Prioritising peace of mind.

(16)

The ugliness that qualifies
East Coast delights lies in the hordes
Of health-care conscious ancient folk
Retired in tracksuits to their shacks,
Or cheaper still to caravans
In coin-slot operated parks,
With atmosphere provided by
Getting out of bed for a feed
Of scallops when the bookies pay,
In cars parked at the beach to read
The newspapers' death notices
And Elvis In Memoriams,
The pages, finished with, arranged
On windscreens to keep out the sun.

(17)

A failed academic career,
Two divorces, lost children, I,
Disenchanted, dispossessed, sit
Out life in Hania's garden-park
As a flaneur, my therapy
These sonnets, bitter medicine
For moods afflicting my derailed
Disoriented self, made worse
Whenever I'm introduced as
Coming from Tanzania, or
Transylvania, instead of un-
Known Tasmania, where even in
Australia it can often be
Left off official, national maps.

(18)

Startled to find eucalypts in
Hania, light sharply splinters through
Them as I reflect on how 'Krauts'
Parachuting in were pitchforked
By Cretans and Aussie allies,
And wonder if I qualify
To be labelled a psychopath,
Since without emotion, conscience
Working to check revengefulness
I dumped Rose with our daughters back
In the Old Dart because she'd walked
All over my feelings for Tas,
Which though ambivalent, at least
Were my right as a native-born.

(19)

Trying to settle back into
Academic life after five
Years truancy in England, Greece,
I failed to cope with depressed Rose
Manipulating me to break
My contract and abscond again,
Her hospitalisations, when
My cold withdrawn mother I'd not
Been loved by as a child arrived
To care for my two daughters, one
Left by my discharged, still drugged wife
To topple off the fridge, a mess
Resolved by me deserting to
Become a bard at King Pad's court.

(20)

Wrote 'Aloyishus': 'Children on
The voyage out drove mad with noise,
Running around the hold in which
You couldn't swing a Cat-o'-nine,
Incessantly demanding more
Maggoty meat, and terrified
When playing they stumbled upon
Mum heaving underneath a man
In corners thought safe from their eyes,
No candles allowed in the dark,
All hatches tightly closed against
Storm-crazed seas battering to get in,
Traumatising them till they died
As much from fear as scurvy's scourge'.

(21)

At forty in the shade kids cry,
Come grizzling round me as I sit
Translating complex modern Greek
In dusty, oleander-leafed,
Dry, peacock-screeching Hania park.
I never wanted them, but Rose,
Encouraged by her trendy shrinks,
Insisted she make good her loss,
Or, as she'd say, 'amends for two
Murders in back-street Paris jobs',
Necessitating surgery
Before she could conceive again,
Curette scars on ovaries the hitch,
And not my sperm count as she shrilled.

(22)

'The Babylonian Epic Of
Creation' shows the rivers as
The monster Tiamat disturbed
And angry when her brood romp round,
Their active enterprises, schemes
Upsetting her as water calm
And deathly quiet till stagnant she
Creates chaos by failing crops,
Brings epidemics of disease,
Obliging her to fight and die
For sloth against her child Marduk,
The king noisily planning to
Improve life, civilise, while I'm
Not sure which side I belong to.

(23)

I pick my pen up, start to write,
Add my activity into
The ceaseless, Heraclitian flow
Of episodes, occurrences,
Events that range from drawing breath
To dropping the atomic bomb,
All links in chain reactions, part
Of an eternal 'progress' down
To hell and misery for hordes,
And now Madge Ripper in old age
As she waits for the silent, calm
Perfectibility of death,
Concludes that Paradise consists
'Of nothing ever happening'.

(24)

Apart from meals, usually held in
Silence, parents shared little else
With me, and even they could be
Withheld as the worst punishment,
My mother closed in on herself
As the only way to survive,
Transplanted from a more refined
Life in New Zealand to fend off
The horrors of Tasmania's West,
My father at the mine, golf, Lodge,
Bookies, pub, football, cricket, chops,
Hungover Sundays, sitting head
In hands as paranoid he wept
About injustices at work.

(25)

My mother seldom sat and talked,
Relaxed and joined me entranced by
'The Women's Weekly' images,
Cooked much beyond a stew or roast,
Shopped, visited, or went for walks,
But listened to the Caltex plays,
To hit parades and 'Pick-a-Box'
Instead of vulgar Roy Rene's 'Mo',
Washed up incessantly and jumped
Each time the kitchen blind flew up
To show a new moon she believed
Seen through a window brought bad luck,
A mirror cracked financial loss,
In bits and pieces certain death.

(26)

As well as going for the milk
And mail to pick up household bills,
I felled trees, loading the chute that
Sent logs whistling to the roadside,
Sawed them on a 'horse' into hearth-
Sized lengths, listening to blade's whine,
Split all into a size fit for
Mother to feed our fire, wheeled them
In wrist-aching barrow-fulls down
A long steep pot-holed gravel track,
Often capsizing them before.
Getting them stacked rafter-high in
A shed with roof that leaked so much
It wet them till they wouldn't burn.

(27)

My sweating hands upon cot's rail,
I'd start by slowly rocking it
To get the first-born off to sleep.
But if she started crying, as
Though in reproach, I'd increase speed,
Till frantic now she'd scream into
My face and I would pick her up,
Impatient and controlled in one,
On a knife's edge as I began
To toss and catch her coming down,
Until at last, thank God, willed to
Something approaching gentleness,
I'd put her back, giggling with joy,
My hanky dripping as I wiped.

(28)

My father was hair-trigger tense,
Exploding into rage if I
Broke windows or holed water tanks
Miming blacks with the mine's steel rods,
The nearest thing to hand his means
Of making me dance up and down,
My mother lashing out if I,
Bored and listless, at last provoked
Her to belt, ruffling icy calm
Coolness beyond 'don't bring your woes
To me, stand on your own two feet,
Tell bullies 'sticks and stones may break
My bones but names will never hurt",
Which was the problem, since they did.

(29)

The Monday morning wash a trial
Because the copper's fireplace smoked
And filled the shed with acrid clouds
That drove my mother out red-eyed,
Tight-lipped with half-rinsed clothes, the sheets
A disappointing shade of white.
I lived in terror of her mood,
A silence that could last like snow
Crushing the early flowers of spring,
And knew I mustn't badger her,
My father in the seven years
We lived at Renison Bell, since
She wouldn't socialise with him,
Ever bothering to get it fixed.

(30)

'Why's Mr Marshall sad?', I'd ask
My father. 'Saw him down at Ned
Bowen's dump. Said he'd come for milk
To line his stomach for the grog'.
'You keep away from him, you hear!
There's just no knowing what he'll do.
He's a half-caste, and the smell of
A cork can make him madder than
A snake thrown on a bull-ant's nest.
They cry like babies with the croup,
And Marshy was born weepy, sad.
Those big brown love-starved eyes have grown
Sharp as a tracker's now he's out
To get at me, the boss, through you!'

(31)

'Is Mr Ward bent stiffly like
A crooked nail from shovelling coal?'
'From sitting on his freckle boozed
His health's been crook for donkey's years.
A bastard of a man. His shack's
Papered with Tatt's tickets, one of
Which won first prize some time ago.
He'd go to Burnie for his sprees
And get so drunk and ill they'd lock
Him in the guard's van coming home.
He hasn't got a brass razoo,
A cracker left for rot-gut plonk,
So now he's back stoking the mine
Loco just as he did before.

(32)

'I saw him kick the engine once
Because it wouldn't take the hill',
I'd continue and hear 'he's got
A tongue too filthy for your ears!
I'll sack him if he can't control
His wicked temper when she fails
To get up steam along the flat
In preparation for the long
Slow climb of two miles to the mine.
He's like a fiend the way he feeds
Her coal and gives her bellyache,
De-railing her on hairpin bends.
He won't be happy till he's burst
Her boiler and his own to boot!'

(33)

There was a student, Beatrice to
My Dante, when I taught at High
School, boyish in her starched white shirt,
Blood-red tie, pleated skirt, shoes black
And shining as wet bitumen,
Whose classically formed face beneath
A beret green as holly leaf
Was far too beautiful for me
With suicidally-low self-
Esteem to easily look upon,
Though familiar enough from French,
Spanish, German, Italian art,
From Greek ikons as Mary mild
And grave with Jesus in her arms.

(34)

In Athens, in '65, my
'Lost' mother's shape stole over me
As hungover in bed I fought
To keep reality in mind,
Hands fluttering over me like moths,
Touching to confirm who I was,
Ceiling opening to soul-blue sky
With a castle of shining ice,
Glittering with pure encrusted snow,
Waterfall rushing down a dense
Shadow blacker than any road
Of asphalt on a moonless night,
My body soaked with sweat and tears
As I became her withheld self.

(35)

Next day observing from a bar
My body swept by heavy rain
Like faeces down a drain outside
I'd dug fingers deep into flesh
To confirm my body as mine,
And so the scary moment passed,
And with it any meaning save
I wept for joy as though released
From something too dark to be named,
But bound up with the mystery
Of mother lost and now restored,
An epiphany, catharsis,
Exorcism of guilt and shame,
I know not to this very day

(36)

An Aloyishus poem reports
An abo-hunt with bush-bred dogs,
A massacre at Black Bob's camp
That never got into The Press:
'Instead of hounds twelve mongrels chased
Six blacks and bailed them up against
Two sad old gum trees shedding bark
That went well with the white mob in
Torn old 'roo and seal skins fit for
Doormats, rugs in wind-loosened shacks,
A screeching flock of cockatoos
Providing the accompaniment,
The bugle notes as ex-cons shot
Them as if they were tattered crows'.

(37)

At Launceston Church Grammar School
I'd helped pin back 'Jackie's' long arms
He'd used to terrorise us all,
While the whole dormitory, as pledged,
Struck once at least, and more if still
Disfigured by his greater reach,
Said tracker to his swollen mug,
Then next day stood beside our beds
To be inspected by tanned-skinned,
Much talcumed housemaster Sorell,
Who kin of boong-shagger guv Bill
Not sure of his loyalties said he'd
Cane the lot since he'd failed to see
His face in our polished black shoes.

(38)

Said God to 'Aloyishus', who,
With a philosophical cast
Of mind was always asking if
He existed, and if so how
Best to relate to Him for help,
Then writing down pretend replies:
'The never-ending sum of all,
There is nothing that I am not,
Though people cut me to their size,
Selecting just what suits their need,
While endlessly I stay intact
As inescapably the lot,
Only desiring to be left
Alone in peace as simply me!'

(39)

'There was a girl, sweet Nancy Paine,
Daughter of Tom 'The Rights Of Man',
Whose image worn by me kept worse
From happening on the voyage out,
An awfulness that fouled our souls,
Those dead from plague thrown overboard
Without so much as by your leave',
Wrote Aloyishus in distress,
Who'd liked her so much in a sketch
By his friend Blake the artist had
Scaled it to locket-size and hung
It round his trembling neck the night
They slipped ropes to sail for the isle
Where noose-happy Arthur held sway.

(40)

'This monstrous ordeal at sea took
A month less than the usual six,
But even so it broke our hearts
With nothing else to do but wait
For rotting food and sleep wrecked by
The sick disgusted with their lives,
The dying wanting one last word
Before released to Davey Jones,
Our right to daily exercise
On deck no better than a farce
Directed by the Captain's whims,
And for solace I broke my vow
To wait for Nancy, starved whore Sal
Dying of scurvy in my arms'.

(41)

'It was an extra punishment
To go on such a distant voyage
Yet fail to see the famed Spice Isles,
The Africans and Indians
Stared at by only those with health
To spare and unencumbered by
The irons the captain kept us in
To curb our spirits hungering for
A mutiny against our short
Rations he stole to barter with,
Knowing of Bligh who'd failed to keep
All those seen muttering confined,
Not one of us spared solitary
As part of his plan to stay safe'.

(42)

'Marched round in single file on deck
I'd rub throbbing eyes free of night,
Shading them from ferocious sun
To watch the heaving, swollen sea
Forever bursting at the seams,
Obsessed by the desire to cut
My scrawny, whiskered throat upon
The thin sharp line that separates
The restless monster from the sky.
Then it was time to go below,
Make way for more to come up in
Their groups to try and lurch in time
With treacherous swells, displaying flogged
Raw backs for biting salt to heal'.

(43)

'Irons wearing red-raw circles round
Ankles puffy from heat, I was
Wed to woe long before we reached
The cruelly named Cape of Good Hope,
My back weeping sores that replaced
It as a tattered national flag
Of red white and blue from the lash,
From speaking up for Sally Jones
To be excused the spectacle
Of men slumped on triangles like
Split open sheep upon a hook,
When pissing on and sea's salt rubbed
In failed to heal and gangrene green
As ship's supplies gone bad set in'.

(44)

'After the mainland shed it as
A teardrop to freeze in the south,
There must have been first glimpse of it,
An understanding that where once
Was just a continuum of land,
A pear-shaped island had been formed
Independently of all else,
But exactly when, by whom,
I cannot get my head around,
And settle for those who became
VDL's blacks, searching for some-
Where to settle, remote, cut-off,
Seemingly empty in a world
As always afflicted by wars'.

(45)

'The utter strangeness', declared 'A',
'At Botany Bay must have crushed souls
Already dislocated by
The weeks on end in wet dark holes,
And now, free or gaoled, there was just
The prospect of starting from scratch,
Safe only till, and that was soon,
They met with desert, angry blacks,
While to be greeted on the West
Coast of VDL by rogue waves
That roaring as though in pain broke
On sharp black rocks waiting for ships
Was to anticipate the Hell
England brought into being there'.

(46)

At Rosebery State School, girl's cape hitched
Above my knees to free my legs,
I fled from 'Boofhead' and his mates
To hideouts in the hills and creeks,
Destroyed their chance of catching me
By taking to the bush they feared.
Among my treasures of all kinds,
From cigarettes and rusty blades,
Ball-bearings, fracture, fuse and box
Of matches to blow up the world,
To marbles and a hunk of quartz,
I'd sit, draw breath and hug myself,
Reflected in the crystal rock
That showed an eagle's glittering eye.

(47)

Housemaster Sorell as good as
Crucified me, since 'Blossom' yelled
Out in anger for looking at
A tree in flower as he taught
Euclid's geometry stuck fast.
He signed QED, wiped his brow,
As though he'd barely step by step
Survived proving a theorem right,
Just managing to parrot it
Without true understanding of
The underlying principles,
The ratios and harmonies
Which I knew off by heart informed
The petals I now suffered for.

(48)

There was a girl, Dante's Beatrice,
An act of mercy in my life,
Who changed my body's chemistry
If looking furtively I caught
Her glancing at me in class as
I taught hungover, prayed for yet
Another day to quickly pass
To free me for what I would call,
Pretentiously, 'the higher life
And my strange destiny abroad.'
And once she brought a butterfly,
Releasing it into my hands
As fluttering and damp from fear
As hers were elegant and cool.

(49)

Assembled on a playing field,
Hands shading bleary teenage eyes,
We listened as The Head harangued,
Claimed 'self-abuse' would send us blind,
Enfeebling further dirty minds,
Debased and shamed our mother's name.
Listless, we watched his injured stiff
Dick-pink forefinger jab and wag,
That stuck up as he caned boys caught
Hard at it in the doorless bogs,
While in the dorm we hung a lace-
Strung toilet-roll necklace around
'Flogger' Fisher's for using one
To find solace at boarding school.

(50)

Chaplain at Hobart's gaol before
My boarding school's, the Reverend Charles
Knopwood-Bramall now gloried in
Delivering young charges to Hell
And earned himself in rubber-soled
Shoes as he sneakily patrolled
To catch boys struggling hard to raise
Their member to a manly tower,
The nickname 'Creeping Jesus' we
Viciously hissed out as he left
With boy in tow to have him 'socked',
'Christ's' back of neck and ears ablaze
As he feigned not to hear a word
Of blasphemy from 'arrant louts'.

(51)

I took you seriously, God,
Preparing for the laying on
Of Bishop's hands that I might drink
Of Christ, my trimmed hair left unoiled
Despite strong peer pressure, when Graeme
Nixon summoned by the Head for
Paedophilia suicided
Instead of witnessing my vows,
One being to purge 'blood' from thoughts,
My vampire-craving as I'd prayed
Alone in chapel for the peace
That passeth understanding, but
Saw convict man-eaters replace
The tale a stained glass window told.

(52)

Chapel Sacristan, Nixon did
Not lay a sacred hand on me,
With just his ghost witnessing my
Confirmation as stand in for
Parents living too far away
From my out-of-their-league snob school
To come, while housemaster Sorell
Handled the 'crime' of suicide
By calling 'my friends the police'
And herding us into the gym,
Sirens beginning soon to wail
Heralding 'Truth's':'The Church once ruled
In VDL by his forebear
Still buggering the island's youth'.

(53)

Nicknamed 'Le Perv', or 'Slimy Dick'
By cruder boys who knew no French,
This teacher coached me in his room
Above 'The Sir George Arthur Quad'
Where we thought homos had been hanged,
And might be still if caught in loos,
'La Poof' just wanting to hold hands,
Massage thumb, ruffling cropped hair as
I rose to leave, his red silk gown
Split to reveal off-hip pink briefs,
A weak white chest that smelt of Vicks
Vapor Rub mixed with sweat as I
Ducked underneath arms flung as wide
Open as Christ's upon The Cross.

(54)

A legacy of shame, I see
Prefects with towels flick at stiff cocks
Till they were bits of candle snuffed
As youths disrobed to take cold showers,
The mocking of a near-dwarf boy,
Who for slobbering as well was nick-
Named 'animal', of 'Snaky' drowned
By jumping in the pool's deep end,
Hands covering his ears to block
Out our interminable hiss,
Of 'Flogger' caught seeking release
With vaselined toilet roll, while
'Blossom' chanted struck my face like
Dog turds baked harder than a stone.

(55)

I can't forgive my spitefulness,
My tennis feud with a 'ciss' whose
Effeminate style upset my
Copy-book, smoothly flowing game,
Until unnerved I lost six love
But didn't choose him for the team
I captained for the premiership,
Deciding that his mincing walk,
His girly, hairless legs in shorts
And pansy way he threw the ball
Into the air for his weak serve
Disqualified him from a side
Of orthodox boys picked to wipe
The stain of 'Blossom' from my life.

(56)

My voyage 'Home' in '63
Took five weeks via Italy
Aboard 'The Roma' crowded out
With emigrants returning scarred
By sneers of 'dago', 'wino', 'wog',
At sharp tight-fitting clothes at odds
With shapeless Tassie gaol-style garb.
Like transportation in reverse,
I bunked below the waterline
That reeked of disenchantment, sweat,
Blocked toilets, and with others signed
A petition demanding peace
From children in The Reading Room
Who'd nowhere safe to run around.

(57)

'Count' Rudolph graced the ship, a suave
Trendily clothed bejewelled 'Kraut'
Returning to Berlin to breathe
The air of European kitsch,
His decorative abstractions
Not on the Nazis' list of banned
'Decadents', since he 'knew' corrupt
Highly placed murderous bureaucrats.
Apologetic for his past
As member of The Hitler Youth,
In Bombay, en route, he returned
To form, shoving beggars aside
And choosing from a bamboo cage
A painted little girl for sex.

(58)

There was a girl, sweet Robyn Swan,
The Beatrice to my Dante, whom
I lost to drunkenness, then wrecked
My life always searching for her
To re-instate as something more
Than a faint shadow from the past,
So thorough-going is the blank
That alcoholism can cause,
Impose upon the beautiful
That only rarely showed in wives,
In women of the one-night stand,
As Don Giovanni-like I tried
For satisfaction everywhere
And never once appeased my soul.

(59)

I heard 'Heil Hitler' as I passed
The Cretan Elders fooled by my
Blue eyes, grey hair, until I snapped,
'Australian, your friend in the War',
Recalling my father's rage when,
Despite his 'Itie', 'Nip', 'Hun' hissed
As we all huddled round at home
Listening to The News, he'd learnt how,
Finger under nose, right arm raised,
Goose-stepping in Rosebery's main street
I'd brought the foreign doctor's car
To a halt, resulting in my
Worst beating of many with sticks
I'd split to start our morning fire.

(60)

Count' Rudolph, voyage at an end,
Toured Genoa at my expense,
Since, trousers round his ankles, she,
The Bombay child, cleaned him out, who
Now crossed himself in churches while
Not looking Mary in the eye,
Drank rough red until dribbling drunk
He was the beast in camps where Jews
And genocide walked hand-in-hand,
His work selling in callow Tas,
Where, suffering from 'cultural cringe'
Few were able to dismiss him
And his 'Art' for the junk it was,
Just decoration with no depth.

(61)

I met 'Count' Rudolph last as head
Of Hobart Town's Art School he'd stacked
With fellow Euro-refugees
Appointed for their loyal support
In purging locals from the Staff
Whose more traditional work was
Hostile to his cynical view
That what doesn't last is the one
Fit subject for modernist art.
Political opportunist,
He found the left-wing Abo push
The bandwagon best to be on
And sucked up by including their
Decorations among his own.

Block Five

(1)

When Pad, hoaxer of modernists,
Met 'Count' Rudolph, new Art School head,
Flash trendy leftist seeking to
Establish an empire of trash
Throughout the island's Institutes,
My hero's Audenesque visage,
Less face than mask deeply engraved
From sleepless nights in deserts of
Despair about the human race,
Didn't slip listening to an out-
Pouring of bilge but answered as
He quickly rose to take his leave
Before the first carafe was dry
By breaking wind instead of bread.

(2)

A victim of 'Count' Rudolph's reign
Of terror in the local arts
Was 'Grizzling George', State Portraitist
And lounge lizard in Hobart's pubs
Without a touch of Wainewright's skill
In showing hell behind the mask,
But given to a gorgeousness
Not too unlike his girlish own,
His 'Renoir palette' quite without
The Frenchman's subtle use of tone,
As gaudily his faces glow,
Flushed soft as his beer-bloated mug
Reflective of the fawning look,
The shame of convict ancestry.

(3)

A nigger in the woodpile, I've
Worked tirelessly to save my soul,
Fled marriages, careers, all that
Would join me to a club of in-
Breds who agree to shut their mouths
And enjoy dishonourable lives,
The comfortable Hobart kind
Where nothing rocks The Arthur Boat
Manned by descendants of his clique,
The early-favoured few free who
Insist that all is for the best
From killing blacks, rainforests, lakes,
To persecuting those like Orr
For daring not to join their ranks.

(4)

In Rosebery's new Communal Hall
On paynights after pubs had closed,
A punch-drunk Abo from up North
Took on all-comers for the change
The miners flung into the ring
Each time the 'coconut' was downed,
His friend his shadow on the floor
Whispering 'stay put' losing to roars
To get up on his trembling, thin
Brown raspberry canes and earn some more
Before the Ref's count saved him for
Next Friday-fortnight to come round
And be king-hit by town's white trash,
Head nodding like a broken flower.

(5)

In Hobart's St Ives I'd drink with
Workmate, full-blood Joe Nettup, ill-
At-ease as owner John Boyes did
His rounds from coat-and-tie front bar
To back, since this sinister, thick-
Necked unhangable local toff
Might, angered by the sight of him
Inspecting my blistered hands held
In his risked after mutton birds
Down snake-nest holes blacker than him,
Just say 'get out!', especially if
His 'piss on them' was followed by
A smile in milky eyes in need
Of scaling clear of cataracts.

(6)

A solitary, bookish type
Given more to drink than girls, I'd
No right to marry Rose, but thrown
Out of Greece after five years in
Vain searching for something to turn
Me on more than dry ancient texts,
I'd come to London hoping to
Regain my dumped Uni career,
And she with money, posh pom voice
Represented the mythical
Castle and princess to be stormed,
Carried off by my base-born self
To convict-founded Tassie in
Lieu of nothing else achieved.

(7)

The cat-o'-nine tail's hiss and sting,
The worrying click in my neck
Growing fainter from life in Greece,
Along with Tassie mapped out there
As a weakening birthmark, was my
Reward for truancy, for not
Honouring my contract to return
To Hobart Uni after leave,
For being physically quite un-
Able to disobey a gut-
Feeling to stay, having escaped
The shadow of Van Diemen's Land
In which, from pancreatitis,
I'd nearly drunk myself to death.

(8)

Feeling deeply defeated from
Ending up back in Hobart Town
With personal problems still the same,
By my position of ring-in,
Prof Crook's insult to Sophocles,
Hesiod, Homer, Aeschylus,
To students of Tasmania
In hiring me to teach their works
Without knowledge of Ancient Greek,
In translations I couldn't check,
My role as essay-marking slave,
Has led me to Hania to learn
The modern language thoroughly
As penance for abetted crime.

(9)

Indebted to a Greek, I helped
Him haul a Christmas pig until
It dangled upside down, a great
Weight squealing from an olive branch,
Then watched him crawling knife in hand,
Pretending that the hanging beast,
Flushed pink, about to burst with blood,
Was being hunted in the wild
Before he stabbed and took an age
To find the jugular and cut
The head off as it looked around,
Catching my eye as if to say:
'You're next for flirting with his young
Niece Nausicaa at Easter's feast!'

(10)

Eve's bronchiectasis drove me
To not practise what I had preached:
Namely, the sublimation of
The gross material world by
The spiritual, her constant cold
Rendering her ugly, removed from
The Hollywood ideal that had
Conditioned my taste in females,
And treacherously I wrote poems
For a smile flashed at me in class,
Destroyed my second marriage for
A new ideal who didn't cough
And cause me to read essays twice
Before I could give them a mark.

(11)

An 'Aloyishus' poem restored
Makes sense as: 'before accused by
A 'Potiphar' and sentenced to
Fourteen years in Van Diemen's Land,
I'd fallen in and out of bed,
Enjoying every woman won,
Continuously searching for
The deathless ideal as in song,
A Beatrice, Eve, Helen, until
Each love burnt itself out, and still
Not once could I bring myself to
Acknowledge and surrender to
Reality, but always hoped,
Convinced next time I'd prove it wrong!'

(12)

Before the woodshed and The Fall,
When Granny's shadow swept across
Myself and Eve as we explored,
My Eden was our wet front lawn
Beneath Mount Black, when Kath and Anne,
The Larkin girls, came there to play
On rarely fine, light-splashed days, when
Pearls ran like broken necklaces,
Were bodiless heads dropping from
Grass stems, hedge, flower-beds until,
Sun setting, darkness swamped by three,
After also perhaps a frost
My blotting-paper soul soaked up
As stars glittering to redeem night.

(13)

Revengefully, although it was
Customary on Christmas Day,
I invited my cheerless folks'
Lively neighbour to their house for
A drink, knowing my mother, cold,
Snobbishly 'stainless', who'd betrayed
Me as a child, would writhe with scorn
Masked as she greeted her, a bar-
Maid on Hobart Town's Waterfront,
Obviously descended from
The Female Factory, whom I danced
Around the linoed lounge and whisked
Off in a taxi for the best
Low-life night I have ever had.

(14)

A narcissist and psychopath
Because childhood emotions weren't
Nurtured by mother, father, I
Dump all women after a time,
Flocks of Beatrices, Helens, Eves,
Then disgruntled look forwards to
The next, no doubt superficial,
Female-induced epiphany,
Glimpsing, what I, last of the great
Romantics, sarcastically call
'My lonely soul's equivalent'
In any chance encounter with
The opposite sex, be it on
The telly, or just in a book.

(15)

My psychopathic tendency,
An inability to care,
Find empathy enough not to
Desert a sick wife and two kids,
Another with only one lung,
I trace beyond poor parenting
To Governor Arthur, role model
Contemptuous of the convict class,
Who without qualm, the smallest show
Of paternalistic regard
Hanged hundreds in his twelve-year reign
Of terror in Van Diemen's Land,
Dispassionately oversaw
The near-extinction of the blacks.

(16)

In old age wanting to confess
My cool, cavalier disregard
For feelings of my fellow-man,
A VDL/Tas legacy
Culminating in Martin Bryant's
Carefree Port Arthur massacre,
I live alone, confidence gone
On how to treat folk and not wound
Them as always I did before,
Doing penance for ruthless shark,
Straight-down-the-line behaviour with
At least one sonnet added to
This epic tale of woe each day,
A therapy that keeps me sane!

(17)

There was a girl, sweet Robyn Swan,
My sure swift vehicle to God,
Demure, grave, serious beyond
All other women I have known,
In her attentive, wondering eyes
A depth the darkest opal gives.
A long thin rose stem with a bud
Beginning to suggest the white
Or red depending on her mood,
A question mark that gently asked
And left me answerless with love,
She touched my soul as no one has,
Bestowing grace as if the Dove
Were hovering above my head.

(18)

Just out of hospital, scalp still
Dressed from his mining accident,
Father in Menzies-monogrammed
Pyjamas walked the line to drag
Me from a Renison Bell lost-
Weekend, enraged that I would choose
To booze with tar-brushed 'Marshy' in
The derelict Jack Grubb's grim shack
With lower-than-the-low Des Finn
Whose gums looked like ridged bottle tops,
Instead of staying home with him
To listen to Bob Dyer or
Jack Davey give the world away
In 'Pick A Box' or 'Cop The Lot'.

(19)

The Torquemada, desert-seer,
Savanarola of slack-boozed,
Heat-dazed, laid-back, no-problems Oz,
Before the cameras Paddy rolled
His eyes back till the whites were those
Of European monarchs carved
In marble for great city parks,
Or was he inclined mythically,
Drawing on King Oedipus, self-
Blinded to better see within,
On wedge-tailed eagles whose orbs gleam,
Briefly flash with love of power,
On hold only till TV crews
As suddenly snap shutters closed?

(20)

Dear wives, you'd never understand
My need to write an epic poem,
To lead a certain kind of life,
Desert the children, not support
Your wish for dinner parties, friends,
To renovate a house and be
As normal as a kitchen sink,
With me despise Tas Uni's style
Of bickering, no research done,
When it's your bread-and-butter, or
Share my hatred of peace and quiet,
The safety of the suburbs, as
Reading my verse you quickly learn
That Jack the Ripper is my muse.

(21)

After our Uni footy match
We drank till closing time then crashed
A party at 'The Pigs', three short
Obese freaks sharing a flat in
Hobart Town's Lynton Avenue.
I ended up on all the coats
Thrown anyhow upon a bed
With 'Dippy', younger brother's bit
Of fluff I lusted after, not
From love or liking, but because
I was a virgin, still without
A girlfriend, and also she knew
About hot baths and gin if some
Retard had put her up the duff.

(22)

My shaky manhood proved, I woke
Hungover, guilty and afraid,
With little memory of my loss,
Aware more of the blinding lights
Switched on and off as overcoats
Were searched for, found and dragged away
While 'Dip', expertly without fuss,
Despite the tangle all around
Enabled me to wolf the fruit
It was my brother's to enjoy.
Worried sick, I confessed my 'crime'
To mother who cooly replied
'Don't bring your problems home to me,
Learn to stand on your own two feet'.

(23)

There was a girl, sweet Robyn Swan,
Whose image I wore daily in
My mind's eye as an amulet,
Who played the role of Juliet
In Hobart High School's staging of
That heartfelt masterpiece where love's
Recognised by both at a glance,
Her Romeo a classmate I
Just managed not to punish for
Looking around at her, or grade
Unfairly, jealous to the point
Of missing the rehearsals, scared
On opening night I'd run amuck,
Prevent the curtain going up.

(24)

Marangoudakis, Hania's bard,
A kind but noisy extrovert
Obsessively in praise of light,
Heroes, gods, bombastically,
In rhetoric I squirm at, has
Decided to rescue me, turn
My boatload of despair around.
Bossed by an even louder wife,
He entertains me at his home
Perched high above the waterfront,
Laughing at sunburnt poms in socks,
Jumpers, till I join him on our
Mount Olympus, compete to point
Out folly, doubled up with mirth.

(25)

Two student-day friends hanged themselves
In nineteen-fifties' Hobart Town,
A third dogged by guilt because his
Ancestors murdered blacks for land
To fatten sheep on, blowing his
Brains out one depressing wet Sun-
Day empty as a church, pubs closed.
I'd loaned him the Greek Tragedies,
And, in retrospect, even more
Grotesque, the mock-horror cartoons
Of 'Fester' and the like in Charles
Adam's weird family fantasy,
Getting them back with spattered blood
I couldn' wash off with a cloth.

(26)

In Evans Street that ran the length
Of Hobart's Gas Works built of blood-
Red bricks, past's reek was reinforced,
Walls jutting out unevenly
Crooked as limping dogs' hind legs,
Jerking as hanged men dancing would,
Barbed wire with scraps of rubbish caught
On strands fencing derelicts' homes
Like scores for forlorn music to
Accompany convicts as they toiled,
Shattered window panes blinded eyes
As inward-gazing on the dark
As Oedipus's who chose night in
Preference to family ugliness.

(27)

Badly hungover, wanting sex
To comfort and console, I'd plead,
Then wrestle with, all but rape Rose.
'You only want me when you're sick
From sleeplessness and fear you'll crack
While giving lectures half-prepared
And plagiarised from greater minds,
From too many all-afternoon
Lunches with that vile piece of work,
Paddy James, who doesn't like me,
Valium no answer to your woes',
She'd more or less rant, weeping, though
Plotting, as it turned out, to live
In London with our two young girls.

(28)

Crete shares with my lost island-home,
Though in a more enriching way,
Because so varied and sustained,
Colonialism, with the Turk
Ruling there for four centuries,
And before that Venetians brought
Sophistication, elegance,
And earlier still, Arabs, Franks, Norse
Made distinctive contributions,
While further back Classical Greece
Imposed restraint, right order on
The vivid naturalism of
Indigenous Minoan art,
Shaming England's cultural dearth.

(29)

Summer well and truly gone, I
Still frequent Hania's park to watch
Sun-shrivelled leaves carpet the dust,
Visitors leaving earlier
As chilling winds blow from the north,
Black branches framing glimpses of
Sweet Robyn Swan's grave face before
Garden's closure till spring and cold
Tightens its grip around my heart,
The Elders now staying at home
To sit over their frugal fires,
Having no Hippies to condemn,
One of whom died beneath a tree
Of Aids, wasted to skin and bone.

(30)

Voyeurs of human suffering, we
Privileged historians, I spent
Most of the winter locked away
With Bob Hughe's work, 'The Fatal Shore',
Venturing out as sunlight like
A faded smile on snow-smoothed slopes
Grew warmer, welcoming enough
For walks along the waterfront
Where long Venetian windows tugged
By time and weather out of line
Were eyes of lunatics that turned
Cracked facades into faces, mug-
Shots of the convicts maddened by
The horrors of Van Diemen's Land.

(31)

I'd come to Greece after a year
At Birmingham Uni with Franz
Joseph Tritsch, a Viennese Jew,
Made Head of Archaeology
As a rumoured 'Baron', 'Count', not
For any academic worth,
Who'd examined my thesis on
The Hittites and arranged for me
To come and learn their script from him.
Instead I taught his classes while
He nursed 'melancholia' at home,
Or swanned around in London with.
Conmen who traded in antiques
Dug up from where no one quite knew.

(32)

A specialist in 'Luwian',
A rare lingo he claimed to read,
The crooked 'Count', interned when war
Broke out, copped flak for stepping in
To Dunkirk-emptied English shoes
As a Prof with tenure for life,
Rode to hounds, swished a crop against
His jodhpurs in the spacious squares
Of European capitals
Before Hitler became a 'pest',
Horse-whipping Freud's son out of Rome
Rather than risk fighting a duel
Arising from their rivalry
For an Italian beauty's hand.

(33)

I didn't stay in Greece for Art,
The Parthenon, icons, gold masks,
But for the history-sodden voice
And joy that drew me, just arrived
Off the London-to-Athens train,
Across a crazily paved street
Into an outdoor restaurant,
Where on a table, chairs ranged round,
A woman danced and hoarsely sang
Theodorakis songs as Greeks
Enthusiastically clapped time,
Intoxicated by the tunes,
The words, each other, food and wine,
And not a drunken oaf in sight.

(34)

An 'Aloyishus' poem declares:
'Our reticence is a disease,
We need a keg of rum before
We're able to get up and dance
Around the fire that usually claims
A brute or two in hobnail boots
And ends the gathering for the night,
Especially if the grog's run out.
What happiness there is folk guard,
Afraid they'll lose it if displayed,
So seized-up with mistrust are they
Socially, inhibited by
Suspicion of their neighbours that
Nervous tics crumble put=on smiles'.

(35)

I hope my epic poem inspires
By showing how in mental chains,
Lashed by shame inculcated by
Officialdom's opprobrium
For my lower-deck convict kind,
I have endured a consciousness
Of being thought inferior,
A policy of disdain George
Arthur, cruel Governor of the isle,
Applied two centuries ago,
Undoubtedly explaining why
I'd fall to bits unless propped up
By alcohol and valium in
The presence of authority.

(36)

Dear fellow-humans born to die
And suffer in the interim,
Forgive my self-indulgence, but
At intervals I need to say,
Clearly, unequivocally,
Much like The Ancient Mariner
For mental health therapy, that
I copped a fearful legacy,
Hands sweating, panic welling up
In company, terrified I
Might lose control and run amuck,
Wipe people out as the source of
My anguish, misery, unless
Anaesthetised by alcohol.

(37)

Out of a sense of worthlessness
Stemming from my Hell's Gates' background,
Reinforced by having no Greek
Or Latin, or knowing how to
Read cuneiform, hieroglyphs as
A so-called 'Classicist', I failed
To find the cheek to take tea with
My colleagues in the Common Room,
And took an age to knock on Pad's
Door to arrange a lunch despite
His kind invitation, afraid,
Even with wine, to face this man
Of authority whom I'd sensed
Was sympathetic to my plight.

(38)

My psyche in bondage to child-
Hood's mayhem in Tasmania's West,
Against the odds I'd escaped to
Tas Uni to teach ancient Greek
History, where, miraculously,
I met Maria Masselos
From Cythera famed for its foam
Aphrodite rose from, who with
Flowing, long dark enwrapping hair,
Plectrum-mouth, slim white fingers teased,
Played the violin all over me,
And because she was in the State
Orchestra raised my self-esteem,
Tautening the slack strings of my soul.

(39)

But heterosexual joy could not
Ever quite manage to erase
The question mark that like a hook
Suspending lambs in butchers' shops
Hung over it, since as a child
I'd been tempted to 'gobble off'
An old lag in the Rosebery bush
For threepence, urine-stinking, soaked
String-fastened fly putting me off,
Though not enough to quell the doubt
In later years if perhaps I
Had inherited the 'disease'
Of sodomy synonymous
With Van Diemen's Land convict life?

(40)

In concrete rot-grey as a corpse
Europe's oldest capital dies
From pollution as Athena
Parthenos, guardian goddess,
Stressed out tries to hold off corrupt
Politicians who every night
Draw up in dark glasses and black
Stretch limousines at 'Café Noir'
To intrigue further how best to
Pack-rape her despite Zeus-endowed
Virginity she so far has
Managed to keep intact, a small
Problem compared to tourist hordes
Who daily swarm her like blowflies.

(41)

Five years in Athens with expats,
Cultured, wealthy, sophisticates
Whose first priority was 'Art',
Meant I, returned with English Rose
To inbred, backward Hobart Town,
Could never happily live there.
In French-American Fleur strafed
Escaping Paris I had found
As gigolo a way to give
Up teaching for a crust and be
A full-time writer as long as
Her neuroses, advanced years, crabs,
Alcoholism triggering mine
Was seen to be part of the deal.

(42)

Like Wagner, not sure who he was,
Grand piano on his broad back
As he trudged round Europe, so I,
Typewriter excess luggage, flew
Fifteen odd times, back and forth
Between Tasmania, England, Greece
Before I recognised, like it
Or not, that from the Hell's Gates' West
I was a Vandemonian
Through and through and should stay put
For my poetry's sake, but still
I know my lot would soon seem so
Gross that again I'd cut my fouled
Umbilical and jet away.

(43)

Travelling to Port Arthur Gaol, its
Namesake-founder the Governor joked
Crossing kinked Eaglehawk Neck that
This unweeded narrow stretch of
Distended track with lash-thin look
Put him proudly in mind of all
The scrawny hundreds of curs swung
By him for good of country, king,
Ignorant on his royal progress
To gloat over his cruel work
That the Devil's Kitchen into
Which he'd thrown remnant blacks alive
Was brewing a future to un-
Do his disgusting legacy.

(44)

A green door in a dark wall led
Down stairs into 'Club Seventeen',
Athen's home for troubled expats,
Including Fleur, whose friendship with
Andreas Papandreou, Prime
Minister-in-waiting, got me
Thrown out of Greece during the Coup
Of April '67, but
Till then when Colonels shut it up
A refuge where friends met and shared
Existential angst, and could chalk
Up drinks on 'Nemesis', a black
Slate hung in full public view that
Incentivised settling the score.

(45)

Booze-dependent diplomats, bored-
Sick wives of Greek industrialists,
Heads of such under-funded out-
Fits as the RSPCA,
International celebrities
Like Rudolph Nureyev, as well
As pathological old queens
Like George George with carrot-red hair
And mad electric-shock blue eyes
From blowing hordes of sailors in
Hania's Souda Bay before he
Came to Athens for even more,
Patronised 'Stalag Seventeen'
As the famed Club was also called.

(46)

Fake archaeologists like Tritsch
Blew in and out, amazed to see
Me thought to be returned to Tas
In fulfilment of my contract
After a year spent with him to
Learn Hittite he knew no more how
To make sense of than 'Luwian',
His professed field of expertise,
And once down the seventeen steps
Into iniquity came New
Zealand poet Lil Adcock I
Ticked drinks up for because she'd been
A generous friend to me in lean
And hungry times in 'The Old Dart'.

(47)

Charles Haldeman, with his novels
'The Sun's Attendant', then 'The Snow-
Man', briefly all the rage, gave me
My ticket to 'Club Seventeen',
And I still weep to think of him
Who also read my fledgling prose
And said I'd be best writing poems,
So difficult and dense it was,
Who needing an ambulance died
Haemorrhaging, since the driver stayed,
So the talk goes, to play the best
Hand of cards ever dealt to him,
A symptom of the downside to
Living in Greece, as Byron learnt.

(48)

In 'Club Seventeen's' mirror my
Eyes locked with death-dark Gianna's, who
Told me her brother died as he
Was surgically removed from her,
And sharing guilt from loss of mine
We shacked up, I not knowing that
She'd left a devil of a man
Who traded on her fantasy
Of re-joining her 'murdered' twin
As Dioskouroi stardust by
Butting out cigarettes on her,
Blowing the ash towards the sky,
And finding me unable to
Returned to the old flame who could.

(49)

There is a girl, sweet Robyn Swan,
My life-companion in the dark,
Whose face illuminated glows,
Lit from purity deep within,
Like my hallucination of
Mother's against a backdrop of
An ice castle set in a sky
Of soul-felt, aching, cobalt-blue
Stretched as far as the eye can see.
Wake, lovely child, strengthen my mind
When dangers threaten near and far,
And help me in my epic task,
Sleep, gentle one, when I am tired
And grown too old to sing your praise.

(50)

One evening, ticking up my drinks
In 'Stalag Seventeen', 'our man
In Greece', ambassador Sir Joe
Gullett, celebrating his wife's
Need to return to Oz, told me
To get a haircut and a job,
And then, about facing, asked if
I knew where he could find a girl.
I took him in a taxi, kept
The wad he accidentally dropped
Getting out, abandoned to all
The dangers of the brothel streets,
Wiped clean the slate, paid off back rent,
Freeing myself to write a poem.

(51)

Sing, goddess, of my search for poems
In the ruins of modern Greece,
Of how one stormy dawn I'd left
Drinking with friends on Skyros to
Pay homage to Rupert Brooke as
A naked statue prudes had clothed,
Stifling my muse as I went home
To a still smouldering mattress charred
By lightning striking through the roof,
The alcoholic priest impressed
And offering me his hand to kiss,
Which I shook in acknowledgement
Before a crowd that he'd saved me
Boozed with him when Zeus tried his luck.

(52)

Drawn by the lively way she danced,
A Greek widow, I lived with her
And strangely shed my skin, caused by
Some unknown illness I took as
A sign to not return to where
My kin had lost theirs to the lash,
To break my contract and partake
Of her vitality. Though she,
Who'd suffered in The Civil War,
As I soon learned, lit candles just
To watch them burn down till they smoked
Like a crematorium, then
Lay passively spread-eagled as
Mine too went out in sympathy.

(53)

'Do you have homosexual
Feelings for me?' snapped Paddy James,
Interrogating as he poured,
Irresponsibly, yet more scotch
To loosen my tongue, though next day
I was flying to London, where,
Rose pregnant, mad with motherhood
Instead of from aborting it,
Paraded her atoning state,
And with our first-born in tow too
Was daily phoning me to come
And bring her safely 'home' despite
Having skipped off to satisfy
Her pride among family and friends.

(54)

'Well, do you?' Pad pursued, and stabbed
A half-grilled steak on Boxing Day,
Having returned, by one of those
Unnerving coincidences,
From flushing kittens down the loo,
As I sat tête-a-tête with him,
Overawed at having been asked
To his home, wife and kids away,
And drinking much to relax in
The presence of 'the great man' held
To be ruthless with enemies,
Passing out in the taxi called
And unable to this day to
Remember how I had replied.

(55)

Sexually unsure men need new
Conquests to put their minds at ease,
To scotch the shadow of a doubt
Until the next time it alarms,
Which is the story of my life,
Wrecked by memories of 'Blossom', 'Ciss'
Revived when someone from the past,
With malice, or innocently,
Can still, decades on, call me thus,
Who, bullied as a child with no
Redress, can become, though a coward
At heart, a bully in revenge,
As in the film The Servant', where
Dramatically roles are reversed.

(56)

My shy myopic Cretan dwarf,
A left-on-the-shelf bank clerk with
Car, house, 'arranged' by friends for me,
Had come lumbering through Hania's park
With a Greek lexicon as gift
For my courting expenses she
Sensed I was feeling weren't worth it,
And giving she opened wide her
Smouldering cat-green eyes to let me
Really see and answer with my
Equally frank desire to make
The beast after eight years alone
As the way to find the means of
Escaping from the labyrinth.

(57)

All places do a prison make
In greater or lesser degree
According to one's history which,
Some bear easily, others don't,
But ball-and-chained by it drag on
In cowed sullen acceptance of
Their inherited selves till Death
Releases them. Though in Hania,
Hidden away, anonymous,
At least my hands don't sweat from fear
That suddenly I'll run amuck,
Murder fellow-inmates as did
Martin Bryant, exploding from
The shadows of Port Arthur's past.

(58)

It's only in Tasmania, on
Risky forays to plunder my
West Coast heritage for new poems
That I feel suffocated, trapped,
'Confined to barracks', as my great-
Great-grandfather, James Sparks, ex-con
Become one of Arthur's police,
If not a redcoat, might have said,
My paranoid imaginings
That inescapably I'm doomed
To murder making me dangerous
To be around, especially if
Someone by an unhappy chance
Should yell out 'Blossom' to my face.

(59)

Enormous, like her appetites,
Florence from Belgium domiciled
In Athens graced 'Club Seventeen',
In fluttering colourful silks hid,
Sailed her obesity along,
Billowing swept as if Queen of
The Congo down the endless ranks
Of natives glistening in the sun,
Lined up for her to choose bucks from
And lavish with indulgences,
Sparing the rest from ball-and-chain,
Floggings, hangings, to atone for
King Leopold, the Arthur of
Darkest colonial Africa.

(60)

I loved Florence's open-house
Style in Athen's Tositsos Street
Before the Colonel's coup d'état
In '67 shut it down,
The mid-morning hairs-of-dogs served
By 'Circe', a maid in uniform,
Transforming us in keeping with
The merriment our hostess swept
The drawing room with like a gale,
The last of Van Diemen's Land's whales
With flesh quivering like theirs harpooned
As we her entourage of drunks,
Gigolos, would-be-poets put
The bite on her for funds to live.

(61)

An understanding reached with her
Industrialist, billionaire
Greek spouse, Florence not only picked
The tabs up in restaurants she
Went to with folk down on their luck
In exchange for their company,
But in my case was once good for
A winter overcoat as large
As any sad clown ever wore,
And for police protection when
The incendiarist I tried to
Save my Dioskouros-friend from
Was briefly jealous enough to
Stalk me and even pull a knife.

(62)

Club Seventeen habitue,
Florence's friend, my scrabble mate,
Hair short as Ingrid Bergman's in
'For Whom The Bell Tolls', manly, gruff-
Voiced chain-smoking Leah bluffed her way
As 'private with no privates' to
Fight in The Spanish Civil War
Till wounded and undressed she came,
Idealism intact, to Greece
To head the RSPCA,
Take photographs of animals
That Noah only saved for worse,
To cure my lack of self-esteem
By telling me that I had balls.

(63)

A midget for my bed in Crete,
Wedding her now a duty, life
Seems to have passed me by, since I
Feel prematurely able to
Write only poems of despair
At having fetched up on an isle
As backward as Tas in its way,
A little-published, self-exiled
Writer who's failed to keep a wife
Obliged to choose and care for one
As stunted in her growth as his,
A discard of the cruel world
He's shamed to be seen walking down
The street with let alone the aisle.

(64)

In Athens, nerves on edge from hash,
Cheap ouzo, Metaxa cognac,
I watched through a street's iron grille
A muttering-mad old man alone
At a cafe table arrange
On cloth white as untrampled snow,
His cutlery, napkin, plate, cup,
The toothpicks, saucer, pepper, salt,
In patterns that never quite pleased,
Forever seeking perfection
That didn't exist to be found,
My way with words upon a page,
Obsessively recombined till
I have my poems, flaws and all.

(65)

No church with Reverend by its door
To shake hands, smile and soften life
At Renison Bell, whose few souls
Were stranded in between two towns,
Where nine miles either way was too
Far for kids without bicycles,
Our Christmases were memorable
With shirts socks jumpers hankies, gifts
To save on clothing for a year
Wrapped in sad brown paper ironed to
Get creases out, fit company for
The tough old chook father dispatched
Before he drove off in his brand
New Chev to play golf for a week.

(66)

On Boxing Day my uncle Sam
Arrived as he'd forewarned to pay
His portion of the money spent
On granny's upkeep in a Home
And funeral in Hobart Town.
A teacher with a microscope
For viewing Nature's miracles,
He'd barely taken a sip of
Plonk mother kept locked in the lounge
Before he raised his voice against
My father's idea of the bill,
Scholarly spectacles, 'old maid's
Thimbleful of sherry' at war
With singleted host's foaming glass.

(67)

Dear Editor of 'Oxygen',
I half-knew I was setting my-
Self up for a rejection slip,
Publishing as you do just all-
Things-bright-and-beautiful bland poems
From the sunny side of the street,
Produce of 'The Lucky Country'
That isn't so for some if you
Care to investigate and scratch
The surface ever so lightly,
The air I breathe from my past foul,
Van Diemen's Land's shadow swamping
Each road I've taken in a life
Of over eighty-seven years.

(68)

Tassie's 'Notes From The Underworld',
My work shares Dostoyevsky's doubts
About the human species' worth,
That as long as one person starves
The price to join The Wellfed's Club
Is too high, and echoes his life
Of an eleventh hour reprieve
From death, his epilepsy, time
In gulags, addictive psyche,
And writer's themes of homicide,
Sexual perversion and all kinds
Of familial disturbance,
Entitling me to make the claim.
That he's my literary soulmate.

Block Six

(1)

Christmas at my parents replete,
Not with affected merriment,
But stressful silences, Eve cracked
Under the strain, bursting into
Tears and speech as we left: 'I sat
Waiting to hear them say they missed
Their grand-daughters, suggesting it
Was all my fault', then criticised
The air of strict bare minimum
Throughout their home, as though it was
Somewhere to camp rather than live,
Hurting so much with truths I felt
Were mine alone to voice, that we
Before the year was out had split.

(2)

There was a girl, sweet Robyn Swan,
Whose long slim adolescent legs
Were speechlessly elegant as
A crane's or heron's as she stepped
To class at Hobart Town's High School,
Gliding as smoothly as her name-
Sake or the angel to announce
The startling news to Mary. Rich
Beyond all women except her,
She's mine to invest my soul in,
To see as tirelessly at war
Devouring the Eternal Worm
To save me from myself enslaved
By an impulse to murder kin.

(3)

Evelyn Helen Wintergate
Were names I married to regain
My treasure trove, having lost God's
Prototypical female to
Granny swooping in the woodshed,
Chip-strewn earth floor the Eden I
Was driven from, while walls stormed by
Bully-boys were Troy's, from which my
Filched peerless beauty had smiled down
Before retrieved, her maiden third
The skew-whiff structure's black-hole door
Through which no child could come to spoil
With family, tubes tied to be sure,
Which I was happy to exploit.

(4)

'The Governors, like those they ruled',
Rants 'Aloyishus' in a poem,
'Were lower than the blacks they shot,
As Davey, third of the line, proved,
Nicknamed 'Mad Tom' to match his style,
The day he docked that drunk he poured
Grog on his wife's best hat and rolled,
Coat and wig lost, up to his shack,
Perspiring, scratching in the heat.
He kept no records and ignored
Orders from 'Home', doling out rum
To keep the convict mob on side,
In public falling off his horse
To earn him an early recall'.

(5)

'Sorell and Mrs Kent as his
De facto 'Queen' installed in no
More than shacks they called 'Castle Royal',
Together showed their monstrous side
By sanctioning the founding of
The isolated Hell's Gates' gaol
For 'incorrigibles', and where
They sent me to stand neck-deep in
Testicle-shrivelling water to
Try landing logs of huon pine
Sent floating from further inland,
To cool my obsession for her
Who'd lured me on like Pharaoh's wife
Then screamed 'Help!', scrawled 'A' in a poem.

(6)

With Paddy dead and Rose back home
Arachne enticed me to bed,
Took off her clothes and trusted me
To love her bulbous belly scarred
By a Caesarean for twins,
Her sagging elephant's flat arse,
Unevenly shaved Venus mound,
Jewels too as aids to beauty cast
Off as I lay, her anxious prey,
Yet waiting still for false moustache,
Black heavy eyebrows and a wig
As coarse as Truganini's hair
To be discarded, but they were,
Alas, all genuinely hers.

(7)

Full lips and sloped-back jutting brows,
High cheek bones, button noses flared,
Uncannily Arachne Webb
And lover Pad the poet had
The features of Van Diemen's Land's
Blacks as they live in Duterrau's
'Conciliation' hung in pride
Of place in Hobart Town's museum
For folk to gawk at. 'Me big chief',
He'd joke, prising open shellfish
'Truganini' bought for our three-
Some's lunch, 'a few months from my grave
Above Cornelian Bay once lost
For want of war canoes to launch!'.

(8)

A student of mine in the Syd
Orr-disgraced university,
Arachne went with dying Pad
To Salzburg during term time to
Care for him writing final poems
Inspired by those of the disturbed,
Drugged, incestuous Georg Trakl.
Infatuated with them both,
I signed her present, let her sit
Exams, submit essays to suit,
But when it came to sex with her
The physical realities
Offended me to the extent
Of backing off and wriggling free.

(9)

From England's bleak cotton-mill North,
Rochdale in Lancashire, I think,
An opposite to Surrey Rose,
In reality Eve was vile,
An artist's moll, a parasite
Attached to soft touches like me,
Fringe-dwelling poet-types who fell
For her romantic TB cough
And nymphomanic, itchy need.
From loneliness and cowardly fear
That Hobart Town would think me queer
Without a woman at my side,
I settled for her, second best,
And stayed married for thirteen years.

(10)

Beyond high-walled Hania's park, I
Take longish walks and disappear
Into the sky's amazing blue
In order to escape the world,
From everything that rots and dies
Monotonously to the point
Of crushing with such heaviness
I fear I'll never again soar
As butterfly or Icarus,
As Theseus from death in Crete
With Ariadne's loving help,
As Aloyishus Featherstone
Into a poem as airy-light
As spray wind tears from towering waves.

(11)

'A morbid outgrowth of the past,
Genetically under-privileged,
Pancreatitically disturbed,
Crazed enzymes eating you away',
Said Paddy full of death and wine,
Bowel cancer speaking as he linked
My alcohol-caused bad health with
A deep-rooted obsession with
Hell's Gates' origins: 'your gut too
From inherited bad nerves will
End you', he all but leered, my mind
In disarray, aware just of
His blue-rinsed thinning hair and eyes
On stalks from sudden loss of weight.

(12)

Wrote 'Aloyishus', 'Arthur was
An evil Governor, buttocks clamped
As rigidly he marched and drilled,
Unlike his pretty son who swanned
Around Amos's huge land grant,
Teasing convicts without the means
Of heterosexual life since their
Disembarcation years ago.
His gimlet-eyed father slapped me
Across the face for buggering him
And sent me for my second stretch
At Hell's Gates, breaking free to stain
With cannibalism the race
Memory of feeble-minded folk'.

(13)

'As cunning as a shithouse rat,
Survival's my soul's essence, since
I lived through first Sorell's, and then
George Arthur's prison sentences
That could have snuffed its flame for good',
Wrote 'Aloyishus' to explain
The poet in him still. 'I used
My well-bred Englishness, my voice
To win reprieves from Jack Ketch till
Tupping the snobbish wives of gaol
Officials brought me to the point
Of erectile dysfunction, when
I fled with Pearce and other scum
Into another kind of hell!'.

(14)

'O grant me poems that soar beyond
The miserable heights attained
By sawdust Roaring Forties whirl
Before it falls, suffocates and blinds,
Half-buries us in timber pits
The everlasting rain churns to
Foul-smelling, shit-soft bogs to prove
That even Huon pine can rot,
Light-hearted, feathery poems that fly
Despite my sodden, clinging clothes,
The never-passing time that hangs
As heavily on my hands as
Would wet rope round my bull-thick neck
Tensed to withstand the snapping jerk.'

(15)

Tasmania's penal legacy's
Evolved to severing the ties
With Mother Country England now
Her breasts are withered and the Queen's
A frowning frump with awful kids,
Di dead and Charlie now nicknamed
Prince Alarming. But apron strings
Not cleanly cut fray messily,
As does the half-heartedly un-
Picked hangman's knot of our more hate-
Than love-filled relationship, that's
Left us upgraded to just oafs,
Bogans not even redeemed by
Rituals of Pomp and Circumstance.

(16)

A turtle stranded in hot sand
A long way from its cool blue home,
The oldest Elder in Hania's
Park creeps down ankle-twisting dust-
Dense paths observed by friends who sense
The brittleness of stick-thin limbs
That might crumble, not cleanly snap.
Though ancients too, they'd do their best
To rush and rescue dignity
And cannot return to their cards
Until he's through the gate, beyond
The scope of their concern to get
Him safely home to watch the fire
And try to dismiss morbid thoughts.

(17)

A Good's Train came from Rosebery
To take us from Renison Bell
Through Zeehan to Strahan's Ocean Beach
To celebrate World War Two's end,
So that bush kids might win a prize
And wolf down food provided by
The EZ Company for free.
First in the egg-and-spoon race, I
Fell in a rotting·hessian sack
But won men's laughter round the keg
And wandered off to watch the sea
Approaching in colossal waves
From far-away South Africa
To break on infamous Hell's Gates.

(18)

We picnicked on coffin-shaped loaves,
Rolled pellets from them to flick at
Mums' bums as dutifully they·
Made sandwiches as dainty as
In 'Women's Weekly' recipes,
Unless they turned soggy from juice,
Ruining best clothes dressed in for
The nature of the occasion,
Or mushy from bananas mashed
That stained through as brown flecked with black.
The men just drank and rolled their own,
Stood yarning and lurched off into
The scrub to lean against a tree
And throw the lot up for the gulls.

(19)

'The evil perpetrated here
Defies my powers to tell', said Pad,
Cirrhotic, cancerous, dream-cursed.
'Though not a cradle Catholic, as
A convert I've their strong sense of
Persecution by Arthur's non-
Conformists and can daily smell
Hobart Town's history of spilt blood
Down by The Rivulet around
The hospital where diseased flesh
Disposed of after surgery
Turned it into a running sore
That's never scabbed, and as I die
Weeps for me like Christ's riven side'.

(20)

I failed to stamp the embers out
After I'd baked a pinched spud on
Mount Black, and later that day it
Burst into flames that made it so
In fact as well as name. Inspired,
I tried to light a fire beneath
My parents's bedroom, but alarmed,
My brother chickened out and dobbed.
Father, as so often, away,
Mother locked me in the woodshed,
Good-suited as for Sunday School,
In readiness for the police,
The Ashley Boys' Home modelled on
Point Puer in George Arthur's time.

(21)

'I can't forgive the strutting Lords
Like Sydney, Hobart, Bathurst, Grey',
Wrote 'A', nib scratching through the page,
'Their thoughtlessness in getting rid
Of ugliness by sending it
To breed into peculiar strains,
Bizarre Van Diemen's Land outgrowths
All round me as I tried to sleep
On Grummet Rock inside Hell's Gates
As one of many herded there,
Unable to roll on my back
For fear that lack of space would lead
To touching misinterpreted
As wanting more than lying flat!'.

(22)

At Rosebery kiddy-fiddler Ted
O'Toole used The Pool's diving board
To hang himself, losing his famed
Size fifteen 'stompers' that just cleared
Wind-rippled water's cringing face
To some dare-devil jumping in,
The same he'd made a noise in when
Coming from work he'd clumped their mud-
Caked darkness down, swung gladstone bag,
Opened to give threepences, sweets,
Hugging me like grandad off our
Gate, greedy more for warmth than treats
In Murchison Street beneath Mount
Black before father called the cops.

(23)

A violent town, Rosebery's men fought
And brought the pub verandah down
With fists exploding on the posts,
War-time hero 'Pissy' Roy Dick,
Attired in singlet to reveal
In tribal-chieftain style pale pink
Scars closing off his left arm's stump
Raised in a mock salute to fly-
Blown Royals tacked up around the bar,
Showing another wound with skin
In ribbons on heart's side, head held
High to protect his felt hat which
He thought knocked off meant certain death,
Knuckling on gamely with the right.

(24)

Assembled in the yard we sang
'Advance Australia Fair' and trooped
Inside to give the teachers hell,
To get 'the cuts' from 'Taffy' Jones
Who aimed for fingertips and thumbs.
Slashed cold hands hugged in armpits, we,
Freed, ran outside for 'Recess', where
'Boofhead', 'Porky', 'Pudden', the Welsh-
Man dared not cane for fear they'd mob
Him for his accent one dark night,
Pursued mad Myrtle and poor Peg
To rip their bloomers off for flags
In muddy trenches dug to keep
Rosebery free of the Japanese.

(25)

There was a girl, sweet Robyn Swan,
Whose face in mischievous, wild mood,
When like a skittish pedigreed
Filly she played in the schoolyard,
Suggested pixies, goblins, elves,
A dimpled heart-shape fit to tempt
Cupid's bow, but possessing too
An ikon's gravity free from
Adolescent capriciousness,
Images I worshipped to have
As an antidote to my flesh
That smelt of stale beer sweated out,
Rid soul of morbid fantasies
And love as Dante did Beatrice.

(26)

The flicks I saw in Rosebery as
A child helped to_poison my soul,
With Jack in London ripping flesh
Of women whose down-at-heel look,
Long lank wet hair, reminded me
Of those young single blokes would meet
Outside Cole's Milk Bar in the dark.
He opened up his gladstone bag
To get his knife as did the town's
Kiddy fiddler·For comics, sweets,
And from a dinghy on The Thames
Immersed hands up to white-cuffed wrists,
The camera never straying once
To show above his collared neck.

(27)

Returning from the Pictures, street
Lights shone until the EZ store,
Then darkness on the narrow back
Track leading to Mount Black and home
Was mine, trees close on either side,
Town's rubbish thrown over a bank
Into a creek competing with
Shit's odour as I ran and fouled
Myself, the Ripper in pursuit,
Ambushing me from every noise
And shape I frantically made out,
While through barely moving rain-clouds
A spiteful moon fitfully gleamed
As balefully as mother's eyes.

(28)

My Uncle Jack, on leave from war, ·-
Gave us a hairy coconut
We hung from a rafter in our
Shed and attacked as the head of
A Japanese, destroying it
In ignorance of other use.
He showed a hari-kari sword,
But only talked about 'the Nips'
If I was absent and not known
To be behind the couch to hear
How fierce sun beating on the glass
Bowl fastened to the gut of 'Herb'
Spread-eagled drove the rat inside
To escape by burrowing through.

(29)

In Hania's park a drugged schizoid
'Cassandra', cursed to tell truths but
Not be believed, wakes beneath oak
Trees rustling she interprets as,
Looking at no one else but me:
'Like Nebuchadnezzar reduced
To eating grass, you'll crawl towards
A stone-deaf god pleading your cause
Of how unjust it was to be
Born on the blighted West Coast of
An infamous isle to folk who'd
No love to give and packed you off
To boarding school for five years of
Complete emotional neglect'.

(30)

The tit-for-tat of history proves
Our guiding principle's revenge,
A never-ending cycle as
Aeschylus demonstrated in
His family-vendetta plays,
Unless the gods of mercy bring
A heartfelt change that intervenes,
The same as higher laws invoked,
Eternal and unchanging, by
Sophocles, and my deep desire
To stay my executioner's hand
As it reaches to wield a pen
Against England's VDL/Tas
Resulting in my scumbag birth.

(31)

Disgracing Plato's Ideal Forms,
Eve ill from bronchiectasis
Was dumped by me in Hobart Town,
Festering from infidelity
With ' Gorgeous George' the sick1y-sou1ed
Local chocolate-box portraitist,
A mix of ladies' man and raw-
Boned syphilitic convict brute
Whose Tassie turns of phrase range from
'You up-jumped greasy-cunted whore'
To one about Evelyn's art
Employed·to·throw me off the scent:
'As deadening as a fanny filled
With cold salt water as you fuck'.

(32)

Eve's student-day boyfriend, a weird
Anglicised Dutch dwarf who became
The bi-sexual curator of
Hobart Town's Arts and Crafts Museum,
Half-playfully, as we looked at
A screaming-mad entwined male pair
In Francis Bacon's work on loan,
Ran one sharp fingernail down my
T-shirted spine and brought me down,
Leaving me to it, having breached
My dammed up madman's hatred of
His countryman Tasman who dis-
Covered the isle, the poms who turned
It into a Hell of flayed backs.

(33)

In the permissive seventies
Eve flirted publicly with me
While painter-husband, refugee
Anton from Austria looked on
Benignly, fostering the chance
To rid himself of her bad health,
A constant cold she lied about
As coming seasonally from
Pollen, not bronchiectasis,
Freeing him thus for Art School girls
Taught for screw supplemented by
Locals addicted to kitsch from
Europe buying his 'abstractions'
And hanging them the wrong way up.

(34)

From Dunstan's swinging Adelaide,
In jeans that zipped down to no pants,
Doomed tear-away Eve enjoyed blokes
Who'd sell their mums for one night stands
With her, as leggy as a foal,
Who shot pool, drove a Bedford truck
As though it were an ambulance,
Rolled her own, provoking the bit
Of lung the surgeon had to leave,
And looking for a 'father' slept
With silver-haired informers, pimps,
Touts, bouncers in waterside pubs,
Outgrowths of a criminal past
That suited the hand she'd been dealt.

(35)

I found her living on a hill
Overlooking Jericho, which
Her 'husband' was crowning with his
Exiled Austrian's daydreams of
Building a castle in the air,
While she wild-catted round, boozed cash
He'd tried to hoard for mortar, bricks,
Inviting toms, including me,
To blow trumpets like Joshua
And bring his craziness to earth,
Abscond with her from 'Adolph's' schemes
To add another turret, tower,
Be king and rule Tasmania from
A structure worthy of the Alps.

(36)

The seriousness of her cough,
The permanent infection no
Antibiotic could clear up,
Romanticised into 'Mimi',
'Camille', the Russian-roulette glow
From her chain-smoking lit blokes up
A dusty, red-dirt track a sign
Obscenely called 'Black Brush',·since it
Conjured up abo pros. With just
Rotten health, what she stood up in,
And a wag of her cheeky arse,
She left Anton-Adolph for me,
Who, by now teetotal, weed-free
Converted her to misery.

(37)

His mortgaged castle, comic nose,
Leather gear, beret, souped-up wheels,
Her silken blouses, high-heeled boots,
Burst-tight jeans, tic tac, sample scents,
Listerine to mask the smell from
Lung disease, cigarettes, booze,
Suggested trapeze artists soon
To take a fall, but quickly pick
Their sequined tawdry selves up to
Begin again as fairy pair
With skew-whiff stars, tinsel, or patch-
Work clowns, who, glittering, hard-as-nails,
Heartlessly break those of the crowd
With hilarious hopelessness.

(38)

At times a vital, clever girl
With zip and energy and will,
At others when the missing lung
Depleted and exhausted her,
A rag doll with a lolling head,
Stuffing knocked out as she worked hard
To cough up green infected phlegm,
Pallor a wet paling-fence grey.
Music Hall, Vaudeville routine,
'On with the show' at all cost lost,
She became grave-faced, spiritual
And rinsed-out looking as a nun,
A violet in the chilling snow
Whose beauty took my breath away.

(39)

Born inheriting lung disease
She wanted to spare others from,
On whose behalf she tied her tubes,
Eve was the child of folk with no
Religious beliefs to console,
And with them was a reject of
England's industrial North shipped
To rot and die colonially,
Transportation dressed up as 'Post-
War Immigration', 'Ten Pound Poms',
To again solve Mother's woes, terms
Still evoking convictism's
Dispossession of birthright, soul,
With all replaced by ugly 'Oz'.

(40)

Until her stamina gave out,
A fellow-traveller, soulmate on
Her version of a gallant quest
For an equivalent of The Grail,
Eve's cultural displacement, rest-
Lessness conflicted with her need
To settle in one place and draw
Upon her inner self to show
That painting could be worth the pain,
Though art's been complemented now
She doctors in chest clinics to
Ease mind's affliction born of lung
Loss, fight for oxygen caused by
A not so 'green and pleasant land'.

(41)

'You must meet Lilian Lovelace,
She's sensitive and highly strung',
Said my shipboard New Zealand friend
Mike Jackson as 'The Roma' docked
In Genoa and I was thrilled
To feel among the monuments
In ancient streets that here was home.
'She's Katherine Mansfield without dosh
In London seeking literary fame.
Like you, a classicist lost in
The uncouth, balladeering South,
Twice divorced by twenty-five, she's
No prude and holds her grog as well
As any bloke I've come across'.

(42)

I loved Lil straight away, her mind
That flashed about in London pubs,
Scorned New Zealand as 'home', as I
VDL/Tasmania as mine,
Slept with her when we'd drunk enough
To shed Puritanism's guilt.
But though we shared a need to try
And shake off the Antipodes,
There were dark moments when we knew
It couldn't be done if our poems
Were to ring with the truth of our
Lesser colonial lot, and deep
Down each despised the other as
Second best for such origins.

(43)

'I've not met one New Zealander
I'd trust', said Pad in killing mood,
As salivating shark at work
On steak and nosing in rough red,
Or like piranhas nipping here
And there he'd strip Dick Spinner, Crook's
Kiwi Classic's replacement who
Despised poets, savaging Lil,
Met at a literary gig in Wales,
As a 'pretentious modernist'
And 'Left Bank intellectual',
Her wilful obscurity just
A pseudo sophisticate's way
Of saying simple heartfelt truths.

(44)

Wrote 'A': 'rapacious, predatory,
Free settlers make their pile from land
Granted gratis by Arthur, then,
Culturally starved, return 'home',
Flee the isle he runs as a gaol.
The atmosphere rotten with hate
And malice poisoned lives produce,
The worst pretending to 'the heights'
Of a low-level social life
Wormed through with jealousies, spite, feuds,
At least one good has come from this
In the despot's humbling recall,
Unable now to favour just
The few who own 'The Fatal Shore''.

(45)

'West Coast louts bent back branches, let
Them go to whip me, stung with 'poof',
'Whingeing pom', 'Cannibal', upon
The narrow, overgrown tracks,
Or threw and shanghaied stones that when
They struck could seriously wound,
Yet sought my admiration when
The snakes they vied to kill were slung
Broken-backed on a barbed-wire fence
For blowies to infest unless
Thrown still alive on bull-ant nests
To writhe and bark like babes with croup,
Kids wild with joy as though they were
Killing Satan himself', penned 'A'.

(46)

'Deluges of sharp nails, West Coast
Rain leaching crucifies the earth,
With thudding hammer blows makes mud,
Sends miners drying out from grog
To shelter beneath tinny roofs,
Where incessantly drumming it
Drives them to drink again for peace,
And with the day-long fogs, slugs, moths,
Mildew, blight, rot, hoar frosts that though
Visually splendid kill off all
But wild-flowers, depresses them
Enough to give up bending backs
To tend the veggie patch, and in
Some cases snap their necks', scrawled 'A'.

(47)

My advent was forecast by 'A'
In poems about a child who grew
Out of the Hell's Gates' goal he knew,
'Shunning humanity to be-
Friend a platypus, while throughout
Renison Bell's lagoon dead trees
Like writhing crucifixes watched,
His soulful eyes encountering mine
And holding me to my vow as
Feverishly I walked the track
To give up going on jags with
Gross derelicts who doctored rum
With meths to curb the shakes that broke
Their teeth on glasses, bottle tops.

(48)

'The boy was strangely tense, as though
Aware that a taut string that ran
Through his being and held him up
Might suddenly snap and he'd die,
An angel of a lad born wise,
Tough, bitter, gentle, kind in one,
With hate to wrestle into gold.
The day I broke down in my shack
I saw him at the window with
Bright sunlight streaming round his head,
Transfiguring his freckled face
Into an aureoled white rose
I held in my mind's eye and slept
Until restored and whole again'.

(49)

Lil who'd spurned me as 'Tas' now binds
With postcards scattered here and there,
As Gilgamesh did when I played
Enkidu, and sweet Robyn Swan
As Beatrice Dante to the end.
We crucify, are crucified,
There is a time for bandaging.
I like her New Zealand height for
Walking with, matching swinging stride,
The pleasing rhythm we set up
Whenever I grow tired of Crete
And briefly visit The Old Dart.
'look', said Lilian, 'do look,
There's Muswell Hill spire glittering!'.

(50)

Do all roads lead to England now
I've escaped from VDL/Tas,
To London where my birth began
Over two centuries ago,
To New Zealand Lil who lives there
Unstained by genocide and goal?
In loneliness I seize upon
Rare cards from her, inflate their worth,
Thinking she'll be the means for me
To write my 'Paradise Regained',
Of rediscovering my home,
Which if it exists anywhere
Must be Blake's 'green and pleasant land',
Shakespeare's jewel set in a cown.

(51)

My housemaster Sorell's niece by
Crossing the floor to ask me for
A dance set fate in motion, since
The twist in my psyche was soon
Revealed as an unhappy mix
Of irreconcilable traits
I in my Uni student years
Had no name for as a Hell's Gates
West Coast of Tas working-class boy
With a private boarding school gloss
That didn't sort well with her blood-
Tie to the Governor who gave
Me shaming goal-bird origins
As a life sentence to suck up.

(52)

My 'love' for Sal a paradox,
Since it rubbed me the wrong way up,
I handled by passing out drunk
At parties she took me to, where,
Not knowing why then, I would loathe
Instinctively her privileged kind,
Imagining my role there was
To be the laughing stock, a clown
Who fell down in a heap among
The local aristocracy
Of lawyers, graziers come to town
For a dose of culture that I,
A waste-of-time Uni bod, was
Somehow expected to provide.

(53)

Mostly hungover or else drunk,
I failed to have sex with Sal as
A horny Uni student should,
Even though she encouraged me
On jetties, beaches, in cars, loos,
Phone boxes, against power poles,
And so she dumped me for a jerk
Who as a lawyer looking like
An undertaker got on with
Her dad, Hobart Town's hanging judge
I feared would read my mind and have
Me jigging mid-air before I
Could say 'Jack Ketch', bringing to pass
The end his daughter had begun.

(54)

I dreaded going to Sal's home
Where her swarthiness could be seen
To stem from Governor William's days
As an adulterous colonel in
The West Indies before he came
To rule VDL, kin on walls
Confirming tales suppressed, as did
Her Uncle 'Tadpole', whose skin glowed
Through powder at boarding school, while
Her dad as tar-brushed monster next
To me so caused my hands to sweat
I couldn't hold knife, fork unless
Wiped first, in panic that I might
Use it on him and not the meal.

(55)

I lost Sal to a lawyer whose
Family as undertakers did
Deals with her dad, 'The Hanging Judge',
Who granted exclusive rights to
Bury his victims for a fee,
Enabling their lad's rise to Chief
Justice then Governor of the isle,
His marriage though coming unstuck
When he, fashionable smart-arse,
Sleazy sexual sophisticate,
Introduced others to their bed,
Leading to her getting in touch,
Hoping for a second chance I
Now writing poems for Eve declined.

(56)

Lil sent tea mugs but wouldn't come
To see me marry English Rose,
Since I was doing so from loss
Of Greece, having bean booted out,
Choosing as well to re-sentence
Myself to VDL/Tas where,
Re-instated, I'd again teach
The Glassies in translation, which,
Still with no Latin or Greek meant
I'd once more teach as a ring-in,
My Kiwi love summing things up:
'Having escaped, returning to
The shadowed isle with one whose kind
First sent you there, is no advance!'

(57)

Mike Jackson watched me down cognacs
Before my travesty, farce of
A marriage, since I knew it was
Be-deviled with ambivalence,
My joy from English Literature,
Emotional attachment in
Childhood to Queen Elizabeth,
London's monumentality,
The culture generally, its style,
While hating too The Motherland
For giving me foul origins,
A history of convicts, blacks all
But wiped out to be proud of, loved,
That soon put paid to Rose and I!

(58)

A private church boarding school lout
From friendships with those born-to-rule,
Entitlement rubbed off on me,
Once perjuring myself to keep
A drunken driver out of goal
For injuring a derelict,
Obsequiously happy to
Please one who was later to be
The Governor of VDL/Tas,
But mostly I was thrown passed
Out in a grazier's shearing shed,
Booze contemptuously left by
My host to help me wake and face
The embarrassments of the day.

To be continued in Songs of a Psychopath (2).

Bibliography

Remote Corners.
Sandy Bay, Tasmania: Twelvetrees Publishing, 1986.

In the Shadow of Van Diemen's Land.
Launceston, Tasmania: Cornford Press, 1999.

Life Given.
Charnwood, Australian Capital Territory: Indigo/
Ginninderra Press, 2002.

A Tasmanian Paradise Lost.
North Hobart, Tasmania: Walleah Press, 2003.

A Post-Colonial Boy (Facing the Music).
Edited and introduced by Ralph Spaulding. Hobart,
Tasmania: Fullers Publishing, 2017.

At Large.
Port Adelaide, Australia: Ginninderra Press, 2017.

An Inherited Epic of Gilgamesh:
A Poetic Memoir Dedicated to James McAuley.
Port Adelaide, Australia: Ginninderra Press, 2019.

Another Love, Another Life.
Port Adelaide, Australia: Ginninderra Press, 2020.

Upper Heights and Lower Depths.
Poems by Vivian Smith, Syd Harrex, Margaret Scott and
Graeme Hetherington.
Edited by Ralph Spaulding and Graeme Hetherington.
Port Adelaide, Australia: Ginninderra Press, 2022.

The Divided Self: A Tasmanian Odyssey.
Port Adelaide, Australia: Ginninderra Press, 2022.

The Persistence of History.
Port Adelaide, Australia: Ginninderra Press, 2023.